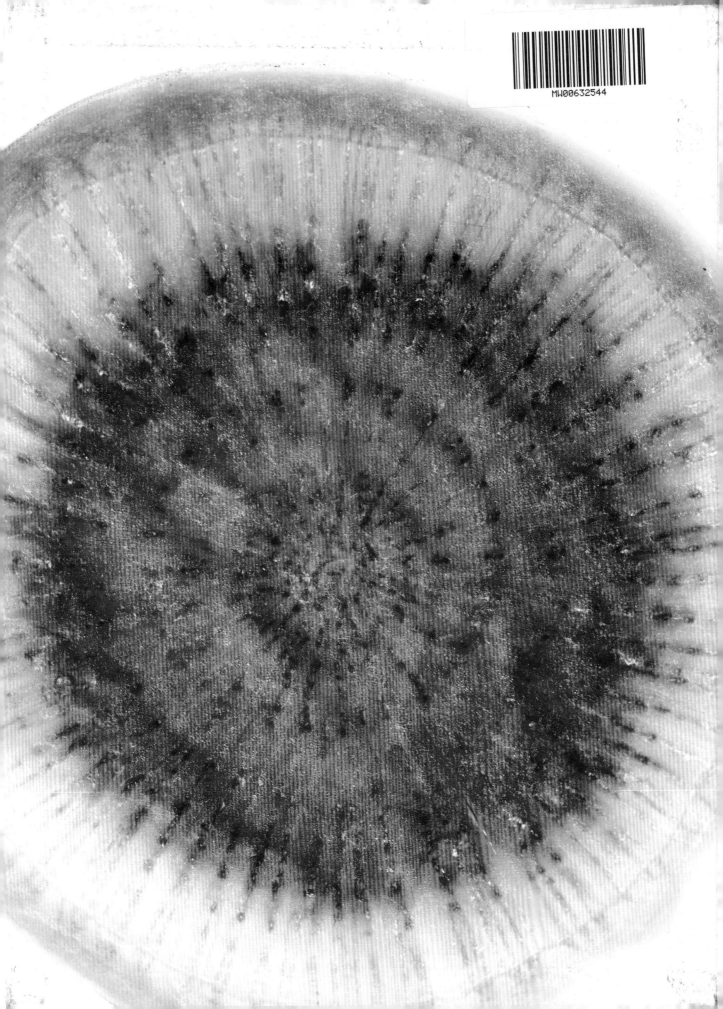

BEGINNINGS

BEGINNINGS

HOW THE PARTY STARTED

MARC WEBER

Photography by John Lee

BEGINNINGS: How the Party Started

Copyright © 2018 Marc Weber

ISBN: 978-0-692-09159-3 (Hardcover)
Library of Congress Control Number: 2018944458

Photography by John Lee.
Cover design by Hope Meng.
Book design by Hope Meng.
Book produced by Caitlin Abruzzo.
Food recipe research & development by Xavier Pervez & Amos Bigler.
Cocktail recipe research & development by Amanda Parker.
Food styling by Lisselly Brito.
Copy edited by Karen Levy.

Printed by Everbest Printing Investment Limited, a member of Times
Printers Group.

Printed in China.

First printing, 2018.

ONTHEMARC Catered Events
47 Larkin Street
Stamford, CT 06907

www.onthemarcevents.com

Thank you to our partner vendors: Bloomingdale's White Plains, Baldor,
Party Rental LTD, and Fleisher's Craft Butchery.

FOREWORD BY ROB BURNETT

Let's face it: most of you aren't going to read this foreword. You're going to jump ahead and go right for the good stuff—the recipes and the anecdotes. Big mistake. Why? Because while most forewords are fluffy, soft and anodyne, this one offers a straightforward and earnest warning that, if heeded, might one day save you from heartache and despair.

Here's the short version: Should you, dear reader, ever find yourself hosting a dinner party, a charity or corporate event, or frankly any other occasion where you are in need of someone to prepare food, do not under any circumstances hire Marc Weber and his company OnTheMarc.

Let me explain.

We all have at least one go-to story that kills in any group. Mine involves a squirrel, a pair of children's mittens and a candy cane. Fear not, I will tell you this story before we are done here, and you will love it. And me. Guaranteed. (Between us, the chance to tell it is the only reason I agreed to write this foreword.)

My first experience with Marc Weber was when my wife and I were hosting a class cocktail party at our home in Connecticut. I find myself in a circle of fifteen or so parents, and I am poised to delight all with my comedically honed description of Sniffles (that's the name of the squirrel in the story). I am a hairbreadth away from deific adulation when it happens: A woman lets out a ravished sigh, "What is this that I am eating?" The man next to her dives headlong into her reverie: "They're little pieces of chicken in tiny waffles!" (Chicken and Waffles, page 83.) Someone else chimes in: "Look at these dainty tacos! They're so pretty I don't even want to eat them." (Candy Striped Beet Tacos, page 11.) And before I know it, my guests are both ecstatic and bonded. Marc's concoctions have magically transformed them into wide-eyed children, as if all are experiencing their very first lick of an ice cream cone. My description of the "hand houses" (that's what I call the mittens in the story—oh, how people love it!) will have to wait for another day. Harrumph.

Against my plaintive appeals, my wife engages Marc for several more events: benefits for the Arch Street Teen Center, Audubon Connecticut, Mt. Sinai's Greening Our Children and on and on. (All for which, by the way, he donates his services free of charge.) The pattern repeats itself like clockwork. Right as I am ready to mention the Sugar J (yep, it's what I call the candy cane in the story—added that little crowd-exploder of a phrase in 1998 to astonishing result), it inevitably happens again: someone goes bonkers over Marc's food. "It's fish, but somehow there's a perfect little zip!" (Yellowtail Carpaccio, page 25.) "I don't like eggplant and yet I'm loving this! How is this even possible?" (Japanese Eggplant Parmesan, page 55.) After every event our guests leave not just having enjoyed Marc's food creations, but also having been magically enraptured by them.

Eventually, I decide I must meet the man. And the moment I see him, lovingly fixated on skewering battered mini-hot dogs onto lucite rods (Mini Corn Dogs, page 71), I understand everything. His almond-shaped eyes and shy smile emanate a preternatural warmth, joy and wonder. I am in the rarefied presence of a man who loves what he does. And it is a love that flows unabated, perhaps even involuntarily, smack dab into everything he creates. Amazingly, he seeks neither admiration nor limelight. He does what he does for the simplest and purest of reasons: to make people happy.

That's all well and good. And yes, you can read this book, follow these recipes and make people happy just like Marc does. But enough about him! Finally! Because at last it is I who gets to take center stage and delight all with a little story about a squirrel, a pair of children's mittens, and a candy cane. Step aside, Marc—it's my turn now! Here we go:

One day when I was walking in the—wait, I've hit my word count limit?! I wasted it talking about Marc and his stupid food?! Nooooooo! Not again! Damn you, Marc Weber!!!!!!!!!!!

Rob Burnett is a producer, director and writer, best known for his role as executive producer of The Late Show with David Letterman. *He is a five-time Emmy Award winner and has received 31 nominations. Most recently, Burnett wrote and directed* The Fundamentals of Caring *starring Paul Rudd, Craig Roberts and Selena Gomez.*

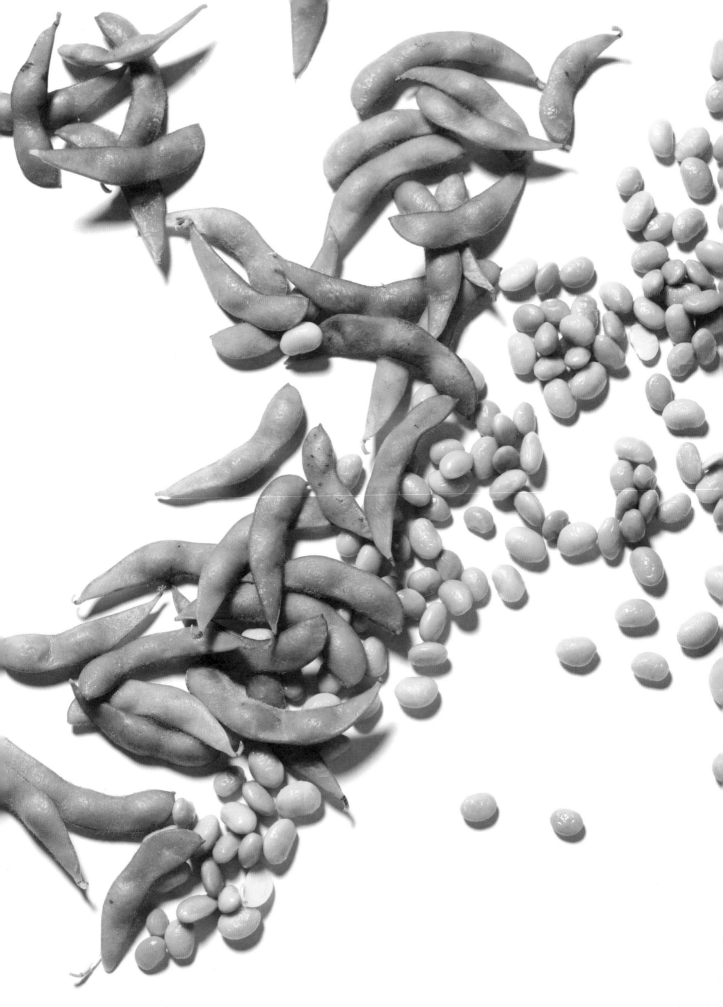

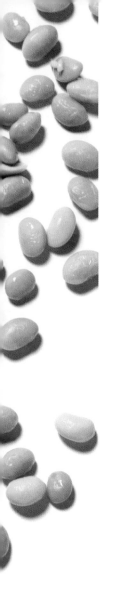

PREFACE

People always ask me how OnTheMarc came to be. It's a harder question to answer than you might think, made difficult by the need for me to respond thoughtfully to a question that has so many answers. My rise to success—to starting and expanding my own business—is an atypical one, which is why I think my story piques the curiosity of a wide-ranging group of people.

I am a wallflower, as genuine and authentic as they come. That's the anomaly, I think, that makes clients, employees, colleagues and new friends inquisitive about my path. Can I say with modest confidence that I am a successful entrepreneur? Yes. Do I crave being in the spotlight or at the center of attention? Absolutely not. I would much rather work a party than be a guest at one—any day or night.

In the business of off-site catering, the landscape is constantly shifting. Instead of building a world for our clients to step into (much like a restaurant chef would), we step into theirs. We inherit the needs of the event at hand and adapt to each situation uniquely. No two events are the same and every new opportunity bears a new challenge. Professionally, we live in a world of unknowns and "controlled chaos"—a term I love to use when describing the day-to-day. It's an uncomfortable place to live for most, but a place where I happen to truly thrive.

As a young company, our strength and happiness is in helping clients host events that reflect themselves first and us second. This unique collision of passion for service with room for adaptability through custom event execution is what has carried OnTheMarc to today. It's why we never ask a client to choose from a set of menu options. Instead, we listen, pen in hand, with a blank piece of paper.

And so, it is my hope that this book, replete with short stories, anecdotes and recipes, will help provide a more meaningful answer to the question: "How did OnTheMarc become the company it is today?" Out of my constant pursuit to make those around me happy, a company much greater than I ever imagined was born.

DEDICATION

I am in awe, time and time again, for how naturally and effortlessly my mother embraced and nurtured me throughout my formative years. I was a lackluster student, much different from my mom. I didn't do my homework, I got in trouble frequently for calling out and I had difficulty focusing in class. It was clear that a traditional schooling path just wasn't for me. Did she become irritated? Annoyed? Disappointed? Hopeless? No, she did the opposite. She embraced me for who I was. When I wanted to go into cooking, she supported me. When I was ready to open my own business, she invested in me.

To my opposite: my extremely focused, truly academic, patient mother. You have shown me firsthand how to be a supportive, nurturing parental figure; how to adjust direction, adapt to new surroundings and follow my dreams. My love and gratitude extend far beyond the pages of this book.

Thank you for everything, Mom. This book is dedicated to you.

TABLE OF CONTENTS

INTRODUCTION

"Marc, look at the camera."

It was 1996 and Mars decided their regular nibble-sized M&M's were, in fact, not small enough. And so, the mini M&M was born. In the spirit of competition with brands like Nestlé's Tollhouse cookies, Mars was hosting a homemade cookie recipe competition where the home cook needed to, of course, incorporate their new candy. The winning recipe would be featured on the bag of minis itself, to live in eternal baking glory.

My mom caught a glimpse of this offer at the store and promptly brought a bag home for us. In a way that only a mom can, she gave me real confidence we had a shot at winning. We sent in a video with our recipe; my eleven-year-old self mostly narrated while mom worked with the ingredients.

"Now we are pouring three cups of flour into the wet mixture."

Together, without any practice takes, we led the would-be judges through our family "mandelbroit" recipe on camera and submitted a written recipe with our video. I think it is fair to say that the name alone likely limited our chances from the get-go, but we still gave it our all.

The next six weeks were some of the most suspense-ful weeks I had known at the ripe old age of eleven. I spent the entire time waiting to hear if we won and convincing myself that, if we did, I would summon the inner confidence to boldly walk into school and proclaim that my recipe was being featured on the bag of mini M&M's. Despite hating attention, this was something I'd be proud of.

I checked the mail every day and eventually a package came. Out came an apron and a kindly worded letter declaring us losers. Ironically, we celebrated our loss with mandelbroit. No one eating mandelbroit feels like a loser. As my mom says to this day: "Everyone raves about it!"

This book is about firsts: first attempts, first impressions, first bites, first sips and the beginnings of OnTheMarc as we know it.

I was three years old when I stepped into my first kitchen—the Playskool plastic variety. According to my parents, I would whale away on the stove and oven with fists flailing and a big, ridiculous smile. Little did they know that their solution to keeping their energetic toddler busy would turn into that toddler's life path. I like to call it fate.

Between then and now, many beginnings have come and gone. I started cooking with actual ingredients in my parents' kitchen at the age of five. I stepped foot into a commercial kitchen for the first time in high school. The rest, as they say, is history.

What follows are pages filled with recipes for small, starter bites—something I happen to believe OnTheMarc does extremely well. Sprinkle in some stories about how we started, how we grew and where we're going, and you have a colorful history of the first decade of OnTheMarc.

ABOUT THE RECIPES

The recipes in this book are purposefully unadulterated, commercial kitchen recipes. We've done our best to reduce the quantities for the at-home cook, but we have largely preserved the authenticity of our methods and measurements. You will come across special tools you might need, techniques you may need to practice and a variety of ways to measure ingredients.

We've chosen to present the recipes to you this way not to make your life harder, but to accurately depict ours. Professional cooking is a team sport and all of my chefs, with their varying experience and backgrounds, contribute to our recipes. To translate them into simpler, perhaps less accurate, recipes would defeat the purpose of our mission. We want you to join us in our kitchen in hopes of bringing out your inner pro chef.

CHAPTER ONE

INVENTION

Necessity isn't the only mother of invention. At OnTheMarc, imagination plays a big part too. Every branch of the company is constantly in motion— innovating systems, designing new menus, concepting whimsical or interesting display pieces and so much more. The combination of imagination and necessity is part of our secret sauce—what allows us to stay ahead.

BESPOKE SERVING PIECES

It might be cliché to say it, but we really do think "outside the box" at OTM—perhaps more accurately "outside the rimmed dinner plate and other typical serving pieces." Very simply, if the right serving piece, passing tray or station display to showcase our food doesn't exist, we build it.

As an entrepreneur and small business owner, I can't afford to allow the design and service of our food to be limited to the industry norms. People tend to hear "caterer" and expect beef satay on sticks and dainty canapés in Chinese soupspoons. That's not us. Finding a way for our clients to experience our food exactly as we see fit not only encourages boundless creativity within my team, but is also imperative for staying competitive. If we want to serve crudités in a hollowed-out tree stump, we do it. If we want to hang fritto misto playfully from a clothesline with clothespins, we do that too.

Our first foray into designing serving pieces was what is now one of our signature serving styles: the lucite taco tray. A creamy, opaque white lucite board, it is long and studded with perfectly spaced clear lucite pegs to cradle some of our most loved hors d'oeuvres: jicama wraps, lettuce wraps, micro tacos and more.

Once we built the taco trays, the floodgates of possibility opened. With an underlying emphasis on clean, modern blank canvases in mind, we now offer custom serving pieces to our clients for nearly everything: a lucite doughnut wall, a bagel display, risers, taco stands, tree stumps, custom wooden boards and so much more. Where these succeed is that, even if the food itself is a familiar set of flavors and textures, the display pieces encourage our guests to interact with food differently, in surprising and fun ways.

MISO COD LETTUCE WRAPS

Makes 40 to 50 pieces

MISO GLAZE

½ cup plus 1 tablespoon vegetable oil, divided

4 garlic cloves, smashed

1 small shallot, minced

2-inch knob fresh ginger root, peeled and thinly sliced

½ cup white miso

½ cup honey

¼ cup water, divided

1 tablespoon Japanese mustard

¼ cup freshly squeezed lime juice

4¼ pounds fresh black cod fillets

SPICY PANKO

1½ cups panko breadcrumbs

0.5 ounce black sesame seeds

0.2 ounce salt

0.5 ounce finely chopped fresh cilantro

0.5 ounce thinly sliced scallions

1 tablespoon Togarashi spice

3 heads Bibb lettuce, picked over and washed, leaves separated

1 cup roughly chopped fresh cilantro

4 scallions, thinly sliced on the bias

½ cup hoisin sauce

MISO GLAZE In a sauté pan over medium heat, combine the 1 tablespoon vegetable oil, garlic, shallot and ginger. Cook for 2 to 3 minutes, then add the miso, honey and 2 tablespoons of the water. Cook, stirring often, until the mixture is bubbling vigorously, 3 to 4 minutes.

Remove the pan from the heat and stir in the mustard, lime juice and remaining 2 tablespoons of water, then transfer the entire mixture to a blender.

Blend on high, and with the motor running, slowly drizzle in the remaining ½ cup of oil. The mixture should be completely smooth and the consistency of ketchup or mustard. Cool and reserve in an airtight container.

Cut the cod into 5 or 6 equal-size pieces, so that you can cook it in batches.

Lay the cod on a parchment-lined baking sheet and coat the fish generously with the glaze. Cover and refrigerate until ready to use.

SPICY PANKO Place all the ingredients in a medium bowl and toss well to combine.

ASSEMBLY Preheat the oven to 350°F.

Roast the cod for 7 to 8 minutes or until it is easily flaked with a fork.

Flake off about 1 ounce of fish per wrap, place it on a lettuce leaf, and shower it with panko crumbs, cilantro, scallions and hoisin sauce.

Serve immediately.

CANDY STRIPED BEET TACOS

Makes 40 to 50 tacos

BEET TACO SHELLS

2 large candy striped beets, each at least
3½ inches wide (about 2 pounds total)

WHIPPED GOAT CHEESE

9 ounces goat cheese

9 ounces heavy cream

0.1 ounce kosher salt

0.05 ounce freshly ground black pepper

ROASTED SWEET POTATO

2 pounds sweet potatoes, peeled and cut into
small dice

2 tablespoons extra-virgin olive oil

Salt and freshly ground black pepper

1 teaspoon crushed red pepper flakes

2 tablespoons honey

4.5 ounces pumpkin seeds, toasted

1 ounce chives, minced

BEET TACO SHELLS Peel the beets and slice them as thinly as possible on a mandoline. (We use a meat slicer for this step.) Refrigerate in an airtight container until ready to use.

WHIPPED GOAT CHEESE In a stand mixer using the whisk attachment, whip the goat cheese on high speed until it crumbles.

Continue mixing until it comes back together and begins to fluff up a little, and then, with the motor still running, slowly drizzle in the heavy cream in a constant stream until none is left and immediately turn off the mixer.

Whisk in the salt and pepper, then transfer the goat cheese to an airtight container. Refrigerate until ready to use.

ROASTED SWEET POTATO Preheat the oven to 400°F.

Toss the sweet potatoes with the oil, salt, both peppers and honey, and spread them out on a rimmed baking sheet.

Roast until tender, about 15 minutes.

ASSEMBLY Lay out a few beet tacos, pipe a dollop of goat cheese about the size of a quarter and a nickel onto each one, top with 1 tablespoon of sweet potatoes and sprinkle with some pumpkin seeds and chives.

CHEF'S NOTES

SPECIAL TOOLS: Mandoline, Piping Bag

JICAMA WRAPS

Inspiration is hard to come by when you're working all the time. So, whenever I get the chance to travel, my primary goal is to taste as much food as is possible. The time-tested strategy to maximize variety is to visit more than one restaurant in a night: drinks and snacks at one place early on and then more robust plates somewhere else later in the evening.

This is how I fell into the flavor combination my clients have come to love so much—jicama and avocado. On a visit to Los Angeles, my wife and I were on restaurant one of two for the evening: The Bazaar, a José Andrés restaurant. We ate more delicious things that night than I can remember, but when I got home I couldn't stop thinking about one of the simplest dishes—a delicate flower made from jicama and avocado. I knew that I had to play with those flavors and textures when I returned home.

The result, our jicama wrap, is among our most sophisticated yet simplest offerings. The jicama itself is crunchy, juicy and barely sweet, kind of like a daikon without the radish flavor. The avocado lends richness to the wrap and little flakes of fried tempura batter—a trick I borrowed from our favorite sushi counter—add pops of salt and textural contrast.

Makes 40 to 50 pieces

JICAMA WRAPS

2 pounds jicama, each at least 4 inches in diameter, peeled

AVOCADO PURÉE (MAKES 1 PINT)

2½ avocados, split, cored and peeled

2 tablespoons minced yellow onion

1 tablespoon freshly squeezed lemon juice

1½ teaspoons extra-virgin olive oil

Kosher salt, as needed

Crunchy Tempura (page 225)

1 cup micro cilantro

1 cup fine julienne radish

JICAMA WRAPS Using a mandoline, slice the jicama to ¹⁄₁₆-inch thickness. Place it in an airtight container and refrigerate until ready to use.

AVOCADO PURÉE Combine all the ingredients in a food processor and blend on high speed until smooth. Transfer to an airtight container and lightly tap it against a flat surface to get out all the air bubbles. Refrigerate until ready to use.

ASSEMBLY Lay out a slice of jicama and pipe a quarter-size dollop of avocado purée onto it. Garnish with crunchy tempura, micro cilantro plushes and some julienned radish. Serve immediately.

CHEF'S NOTES

SPECIAL TOOLS: Mandoline, Piping Bag, Deep Fryer

BLACKENED COD TACOS

Makes 40 to 50 tacos

CAJUN AIOLI (MAKES 1 PINT)

12 ounces Homemade Mayonnaise (page 214)

0.5 ounce Blackening Seasoning (page 222), toasted

2½ teaspoons freshly squeezed lime juice

CRUNCHY CABBAGE SLAW

5 cups thinly sliced or shredded green cabbage

2 cups thinly sliced or shredded red cabbage

1 cup grated carrot

3 tablespoons freshly squeezed lime juice

Kosher salt

COD

1 pound cod fillets

Salt

½ cup Blackening Seasoning (page 222)

40 to 50 (3-inch) corn tortillas

1 cup roughly chopped cilantro leaves or micro cilantro plushes

4 to 6 limes, cut into wedges

CAJUN AIOLI Combine all the ingredients in a mixing bowl and whisk until fully incorporated. Transfer the aioli to an airtight container and refrigerate.

CRUNCHY CABBAGE SLAW Place the vegetables in a large bowl, add the lime juice and toss well to combine, then taste the slaw and season with salt as desired. Cover and refrigerate the slaw until ready to use.

COD Lay the cod on a parchment-lined baking sheet. Season the top of each fillet generously with salt and the blackening seasoning, then cover the baking sheet with plastic wrap and refrigerate for 3 to 4 hours.

Preheat the oven to 350°F.

Remove the cod from the refrigerator, unwrap the baking sheet and bake for 7 to 8 minutes or until the fish flakes easily with a fork.

Remove the cod from the oven and tent it with foil.

ASSEMBLY Lay out the corn tortillas on a warm griddle and flake a bit of cod into each one.

After 2 minutes, remove the tacos and garnish with some crunchy slaw, a drizzle of aioli and a sprinkle of cilantro. Serve with the lime wedges.

Serve immediately.

CHEF'S NOTES

You can use a 3-inch cookie cutter to cut the tortillas down to bite size, but this recipe works great for regular 5- or 6-inch tacos, too.

SUMMER SQUASH TACOS

Makes 40 to 50 pieces

SPICY GARLIC CREMA

1 cup sour cream

1 cup heavy cream

1 teaspoon salt

3 garlic cloves, grated

SQUASH SLAW

4.5 ounces zucchini, julienned

4.5 ounces yellow squash, julienned

2 teaspoons finely chopped fresh mint

3 tablespoons freshly squeezed lemon juice

¼ cup extra-virgin olive oil

0.2 ounce salt

3 quarts vegetable oil, for frying

40 to 50 squash blossoms

1 recipe Tempura Batter (page 224)

40 to 50 (3-inch) corn tortillas

4 scallions, thinly sliced

6 ounces queso blanco, crumbled

SPICY GARLIC CREMA Combine all the ingredients in a bowl and refrigerate until ready to use.

SQUASH SLAW Toss all the ingredients together in a large bowl about 15 minutes before serving.

ASSEMBLY Heat the vegetable oil in a deep fryer to 350°F.

Dip each squash blossom into the tempura batter, shake off any excess and carefully drop it into the hot oil. Fry the squash blossoms 3 or 4 at a time for 45 seconds or until golden brown. Transfer to a paper towel-lined plate to drain.

While the squash blossoms are frying, start heating the tortillas on a warm griddle.

In each warm tortilla, put one fried squash blossom, some squash slaw and a drizzle of garlic crema. Garnish with the scallions and queso blanco and serve warm.

CHEF'S NOTES

SPECIAL TOOLS: Deep Fryer

CHAPTER TWO

BARING ALL

It probably comes as no surprise that my bar mitzvah
was food-focused. When all the other kids wanted
(and had) huge theme parties with sliders, fries,
dancing, games and branded favors, I didn't. I wanted
a sushi party. I asked for a sushi chef to teach me and
my six friends how to make sushi in my parents'
house—that's it. Two things drove this request: my
subtle timidity for being the center of attention and my
budding love for creating food. In hindsight, it was
actually bolder than I imagined—to have broken the
mitzvah mold. In hindsight, that boldness—to plainly be
myself and do what I love—has carried me to today.

SPICY TUNA ON CRISPY RICE

Nothing makes my wife, Erica, happier than introducing someone to food she's excited about. This played into the early days of our relationship—significantly when we were doing our best to eat every delicious thing in New York. Before Erica introduced me to it, I had never heard of this combination of crispy rice topped with spiced fish. We had it at Koi in New York on one of our first dates, then ate it at Isaka-Ya on a trip to LA. After another meal together, when we had it at Nobu, I knew we had to make it at OnTheMarc.

The thing that makes this dish great is the mixture of texture, temperature and flavor. The tuna should be cold and the rice should be hot. When we make it we always use sushi-grade Ahi tuna, but, to be completely honest, the real star is the hot, chewy rice. It's one of our most popular items and, personally, I love it. Erica, you were right.

Makes 40 to 50 pieces

SPICY MAYO

1 recipe Homemade Mayonnaise (page 214)

5.25 ounces Sriracha

0.15 ounce kosher salt

CRISPY RICE

2 cups sushi rice

3 tablespoons sweet soy sauce

3 tablespoons rice wine vinegar

2¼ cups water

Pinch of salt

1 pound sushi-grade tuna, skin removed

3 quarts vegetable oil, for frying

4 scallions, thinly sliced

⅓ cup sesame seeds

SPICY MAYO In a small bowl, whisk together the mayo, Sriracha and salt until combined. Transfer to an airtight container and refrigerate until ready to use.

CRISPY RICE Preheat the oven to 350°F. Place the sushi rice in a fine-mesh strainer and rinse it until the water runs clear.

Dump the rice into a 9 x 13-inch baking dish and add the sweet soy sauce, rice wine vinegar, water and salt. Stir the mixture well to incorporate everything.

Shake the pan to distribute the rice evenly, then cover the rice with a sheet of parchment paper and wrap the pan tightly with aluminum foil.

Bake the rice for 22 to 25 minutes or until tender. Take the baking dish out of the oven and remove the parchment and foil.

With a spatula, press the rice into a thick, level layer, about ¾ inch thick (you can also use a small baking dish to press the rice; grease the bottom and sides with cooking spray for this step).

CONTINUED >

Let the rice cool to room temperature, then cover and refrigerate overnight.

The day of the party, using a paring knife, cut vertical and horizontal lines into the rice cake so that you end up with 40 to 50 1¼-inch squares. Use a spatula to remove the squares from the baking dish.

TUNA Prepare the tuna no more than 1 hour before your party begins. Make sure the tuna is completely clean (no scales or skin); remove and discard the bloodline.

Cut the tuna into a few smaller pieces to make it easier to work with, then dice it into ¼-inch cubes.

Transfer the tuna to an airtight container and refrigerate until ready to use.

ASSEMBLY Heat the vegetable oil in your deep fryer to 350°F.

In a small bowl, mix the tuna with 4 to 5 tablespoons of the spicy mayo and season with salt.

Throw a few rice squares into the fryer and cook for 2 minutes or until they are golden brown.

Remove the fried rice squares, using a slotted spoon, and transfer them to a paper towel-lined plate to drain. Repeat with the remaining rice squares. Put 1 tablespoon of the tuna mixture on each rice square and sprinkle with scallions and sesame seeds.

Serve immediately.

SPECIAL TOOLS: Deep Fryer

PRO TIP: Put your container of tuna in a bowl of ice water to keep it cold during assembly.

YELLOWTAIL CARPACCIO

When ingredients are best simply prepared, in all of their raw honesty, we try not to interrupt that taste experience with too much technique or additional flavor profiles. Some ingredients, like perfectly fresh high-quality tuna, are just not meant to be altered much.

Served on our collection of Himalayan salt blocks, this carpaccio is an OTM fan favorite. Salt blocks lend even seasoning to the fish that is hard to replicate by hand. The fatty fish needs this even salinity to exhibit its flavor. This canapé is almost too easy and so beautiful in all of its bareness.

Makes 50 pieces

2 pounds yellowtail or hamachi, cut into
⅛- to ⅙-inch-thick slices

Salt block, available at specialty culinary stores
or Amazon.com

4 ounces jicama, peeled and julienned

1 pomelo, peeled and cut into 50 bite-size pieces

1–2 ounces micro chive sprouts (can be substituted
with chives in a pinch)

Zest of 2 lemons

Extra-virgin olive oil, as needed

ASSEMBLY Lay a few slices of tuna on the salt block.

Place some jicama, a pomelo segment and a sprinkle of chives or chive sprouts (seen here) on each piece of tuna.

Sprinkle the tuna with the lemon zest, roll it shut and skewer at a diagonal angle for easy grabbing. Drizzle lightly with olive oil just before serving.

Serve immediately.

CHEF'S NOTES

When preparing this dish, remember to oil your salt block to create a buffer for your fish, otherwise the moisture of the fish in direct contact with the salt block may create a brine and overdo the salt. Plan to only keep the fish on the block for a few minutes.

Feel free to subsitute your favorite citrus fruit— or use a combination, pictured here.

SPECIAL TOOLS: Salt Block, 50 Cocktail Skewers

SHRIMP CEVICHE

Makes 50 pieces

CEVICHE

1½ pounds fresh shrimp (31 to 40), peeled
and deveined, tails removed

½ lime

2 garlic cloves, crushed

1 shallot, thinly sliced

5 ounces finely diced mango

2.5 ounces unsweetened shredded coconut

5 ounces finely diced jicama

2 tablespoons extra-virgin olive oil

5 ounces finely diced avocado

4 tablespoons freshly squeezed lime juice

TARO CHIPS

3 quarts vegetable oil, for frying

1 pound taro root

2 tablespoons chopped fresh cilantro

CEVICHE Bring a medium pot of salted water to a boil. Prepare an ice bath.

Slice each shrimp lengthwise down the middle so that you have two matching halves. Place the shrimp in a bowl with the lime half, crushed garlic and sliced shallot. Pour in enough boiling water to cover the shrimp, about 4 cups.

When the shrimp are opaque and cooked through, use a slotted spoon to transfer them to the ice bath to set the color and stop the cooking.

Drain the shrimp, transfer to a clean, nonreactive bowl, and add the mango, coconut, jicama and olive oil. Toss well to combine. Five minutes before serving, add the avocado and lime juice; toss well.

TARO CHIPS Heat the oil in a deep fryer to 325°F. Slice the taro ¹⁄₁₆ inch thick on a mandoline.

Fry the taro chips in batches for 1 minute or until light golden brown. Remove the taro chips from the deep fryer, using a slotted spoon, and transfer them to a paper towel-lined plate to drain.

ASSEMBLY Place 1 tablespoon of the ceviche on each taro chip, shower with fresh chopped cilantro and serve immediately.

CHEF'S NOTES

SPECIAL TOOLS: Mandoline, Deep Fryer

TO ETHAN:
HOW I MET YOUR MOTHER

Three things were getting in the way of me finding a girlfriend: living in my parents' basement, living in Stamford, Connecticut, and working all the time. If you've never worked in hospitality, you have no idea how hard it is to meet people during your time off, which is either weekday mornings or never. JDate seemed like my only hope.

One night, after a long day of cooking, I came home to a message from a girl in a cookie monster costume. She wore the costume so unapologetically with the most genuine smile. We hadn't even met yet and already I was smitten. We chatted back and forth about our lives and food and wine and, eventually, made plans for a date.

Erica ("E") lived in Manhattan and made reservations for us at The Rusty Knot. We bonded over pretzel dogs, Sloppy Joes and a couple rounds of Dark 'n Stormys. One gastronomic date led to another and, before I knew it, we were tasting NYC together and falling in love. Against all odds, I did it. I found my best friend and future wife. Despite the fact that food is my career and cooking is what I do, Erica's love for food and drink far exceeds mine. This fact alone was enough to say "I do" only a year and a half after we met.

SEARED BAY SCALLOP CEVICHE

Makes 40 to 50 pieces

ROASTED CORN SALAD (MAKES 3 CUPS)

2 cups fresh sweet corn kernels

2 teaspoons salt

Extra-virgin olive oil

½ cup finely diced red bell pepper

½ small red onion, finely diced

Zest and juice of 1 lime

1 teaspoon finely chopped fresh cilantro

1 cup thinly sliced hearts of palm

SCALLOPS

Extra-virgin olive oil

2 pounds bay scallops (80 to 100 total), shells removed and set aside

Zest and juice of 1 lime

Salt and freshly ground black pepper

3 scallions, thinly sliced

ROASTED CORN SALAD Place a rimmed baking sheet on the center rack of the oven and preheat to 425°F.

In a medium bowl, toss the corn kernels with the salt and enough olive oil to coat them.

Spread the corn in an even layer on the preheated baking sheet and roast for 5 to 7 minutes, until golden brown. Remove from the oven and set aside to cool.

Once the corn has cooled to room temperature, place it in a large mixing bowl along with the bell pepper, onion, lime zest and juice, cilantro and hearts of palm.

Toss with a sprinkle of salt and a drizzle of olive oil, taste and adjust the seasonings as desired. Cover and refrigerate until ready to use.

SCALLOPS Place a medium sauté pan over medium-high heat. When the pan is hot, add some olive oil and a handful of scallops. Sauté the scallops for 45 seconds, add some lime zest and juice, season with salt and pepper and toss to flip the scallops. Cook for another 45 seconds, then immediately remove the pan from the heat. Repeat with the remaining scallops.

ASSEMBLY In each scallop shell, place 1 or 2 scallops (depending on size), about 2 tablespoons of the corn salad and a garnish of sliced scallions.

Serve immediately.

CHOOSING A NAME

"It should be something catchy; maybe something like OnTheMarc? But not… because that's corny."

My older brother, though easy going, has always had strong opinions. I like to remind him of that personality trait every now and again, in the same way he likes to accuse me of being high maintenance. A marketing maven and brand consultant at the time, Ian decided it was in my best interest to call the company something with my name in it. We came up with a list together—some with my name, some without it. We netted out right where our conversation began: OnTheMarc.

OnTheMarc is my life. It's me. If I was going to give myself and my life over to something I believed in so much, for better or worse, it may as well have my name in it.

VADOUVAN LAMB CRUDO

In Westport, a short drive from our kitchen in Stamford, Connecticut, is a fantastic butcher which sources only whole, pasture-raised animals. Their local lamb was the inspiration for this globally spiced dish. Naturally, because you're going to be eating this meat raw, it's best to seek out a similar butcher close to you, or at least buy the best-quality meat you can find.

Makes 40 to 50 pieces

PAPADUMS

4 cups lentil flour

½ teaspoon freshly ground black pepper

½ teaspoon ground cumin

¼ teaspoon salt

2 tablespoons water

3 quarts vegetable oil, for frying

LAMB

3 pounds lamb loin, very finely chopped

3 tablespoons olive oil

2 tablespoons freshly squeezed lemon juice

1 cup plain, whole-fat Greek yogurt

3 tablespoons Vadouvan Spice Blend (page 223)

12 quail egg yolks

2 radishes, shaved

Pickled Shallots (page 221)

PAPADUMS Preheat the oven to 200°F.

Mix together the lentil flour, black pepper, cumin, salt and water in a standing mixer on medium speed until a smooth dough forms. You may have to add more water by the teaspoon until the dough comes together.

Roll the dough into a $\frac{1}{16}$-inch-thick sheet and cut it into 40 to 50 rounds using a 2-inch biscuit or cookie cutter.

Place the rounds on baking sheets and dehydrate them in the oven for 1 hour. Remove the papadums from the oven and set them aside to cool.

Heat the oil in a deep fryer to 325°F and fry the papadums in batches for 45 seconds or until crispy. Remove with a slotted spoon and drain on paper towel-lined plates.

LAMB Mix together the lamb, olive oil, lemon juice and yogurt in an airtight container. Refrigerate for 1 hour. Add the vadouvan spice blend and egg yolks to the marinated lamb and stir to combine.

ASSEMBLY Scoop about 1½ tablespoons of the lamb mixture onto each fried papadum. Garnish each with a piece of shaved radish and a piece of pickled shallot. Serve immediately.

CHEF'S NOTES

Reserve 2 or 3 yolks for garnish if you plan to serve this family style, as pictured.

SPECIAL TOOLS: Deep Fryer, 2-Inch Biscuit Cutter

CHAPTER THREE

AN EDUCATION

Before the second grade I was learning fundamental cooking techniques from my mom, an avid home cook and reader of *Gourmet* and *Bon Appétit.* We would make dinner together frequently and I became a tiny chef who could sauté, steam and stir-fry.

Fast-forward to high school graduation and I was on my way to the Culinary Institute of America in Hyde Park, New York, known informally as the "Harvard of Cooking Schools." The small campus played a large part in my decision to go there. If you asked me then whether it was well worth my time, I'd ignorantly exclaim that it wasn't. By the time I got to culinary school I had quite a bit of experience under my belt for an eighteen-year-old— almost four years—and I knew it all (or so I thought).

My education at the CIA was, however, copious. I learned about ego and modesty, about the importance of continuing to learn throughout my entire life and, of course, the industry standard skills and lingo necessary to cut my teeth in professional kitchens as a trained chef.

And that wouldn't be the last of it.

FOUR SEASONS
RICE PAPER ROLLS

I began making and serving summer rolls at the onset of OnTheMarc. They're technical, beautiful and one of the ways I like to educate myself and my clients about the rhythm of the seasons. They're also a fantastic option for your vegan and vegetarian guests!

The translucence of the rice paper offers a glimpse into the filling; whatever you choose, may it be colorful. Rice paper rolls are also a fun way to play with texture and whatever else you love. If I had to choose the most inspiring canvas for creative hors d'oeuvres, this would be it.

SESAME HALIBUT ROLL WITH SPICY PEANUT SAUCE

Makes 49 pieces

PEANUT DIPPING SAUCE

⅔ cup smooth peanut butter

2 garlic cloves, grated

¼ cup lime juice

¼ cup soy sauce

2 teaspoons sugar

¼ teaspoon cayenne pepper

⅔ cup water

HALIBUT

½ cup tahini

½ cup honey

⅓ cup water

4 pounds halibut

MUSHROOMS

1 pound trumpet mushrooms

Extra-virgin olive oil

Salt

7 sheets rice paper

5.25 ounces shredded bok choy

5.5 ounces grated daikon radish

½ cup chopped fresh cilantro

Pickled Kumquat (page 220)

PEANUT DIPPING SAUCE In a medium bowl, whisk together all the dipping sauce ingredients until thoroughly combined. Cover and refrigerate until needed.

HALIBUT Preheat the oven to 350°F and line a baking sheet with parchment paper. In a small bowl, whisk together the tahini, honey and water. Brush this mixture all over the halibut, place the fish on the prepared baking sheet and roast for 10 to 12 minutes. Remove from the oven, let the fish cool, then flake it apart.

MUSHROOMS Slice the trumpet mushrooms into ⅛-inch-thick rounds. Place them on a rimmed baking sheet, toss with extra-virgin olive oil and salt, and roast for 6 minutes or until tender. Cool and reserve.

ASSEMBLY Wet a rice paper wrapper with hot water until just pliable. Lay it on a cutting board and add layers of fish, bok choy, mushrooms, radish, cilantro and a few slices of kumquats. Roll tightly. Cover with a damp tea towel and repeat with the remaining wrappers and fillings.

Cut each roll into 7 equal pieces and serve with the peanut sauce on the side.

VIETNAMESE SUMMER ROLLS

Makes 49 pieces

CILANTRO SAUCE

1 garlic clove, smashed

0.25 ounce thinly sliced jalapeño pepper

2 cups fresh cilantro leaves

2 ounces mirin

5 teaspoons honey

5 ounces rice wine vinegar

1 tablespoon Dijon mustard

Salt

½ cup ice cubes

2 cups vegetable oil

7 sheets rice paper

5.25 ounces grated carrot

5.25 ounces julienned cucumber

5.25 ounces shredded napa cabbage

1 cup chopped fresh cilantro

14 to 21 fresh basil leaves

5.25 ounces Pickled Red Onions (page 221)

CILANTRO SAUCE Combine all the ingredients except the oil in a blender. Blend on high speed until smooth, then, with the motor running, slowly stream in the olive oil. Transfer the sauce to an airtight container and refrigerate until needed.

ASSEMBLY Wet a rice paper wrapper with hot water until just pliable. Lay it on a cutting board and add layers of carrot, cucumber, cabbage, cilantro, basil and pickled onion. Roll tightly. Cover with a damp tea towel and repeat with the remaining wrappers and fillings.

Cut each roll into 7 equal pieces and serve with the cilantro sauce on the side.

VIETNAMESE SUMMER ROLLS WITH 5-SPICE SEARED DUCK

Makes 56 pieces

5-SPICE SEARED DUCK

1 tablespoon ground cinnamon

1 tablespoon ground star anise

1¼ teaspoons ground fennel seeds

1¼ teaspoons ground Szechuan pepper

¼ teaspoon ground cloves

1 tablespoon salt

1 (8-ounce) magret duck breast

NUOC CHAM SAUCE

¾ cup freshly squeezed lime juice

6 tablespoons fish sauce

½ cup packed brown sugar

1 cup water

2 garlic cloves, grated

1 Thai bird chile, minced

8 sheets rice paper

5.25 ounces grated carrot

5.25 ounces julienned cucumber

5.25 ounces shredded napa cabbage

1 cup chopped fresh cilantro

16 to 24 leaves fresh basil

5.25 ounces Pickled Red Onions (page 221)

DUCK In a small bowl, mix together the cinnamon, star anise, fennel seeds, Szechuan pepper, cloves and salt. Dust the duck breast all over with 2 tablespoons of this spice blend, then place it in an airtight container and refrigerate overnight.

The next day, preheat the oven to 350°F.

Place the duck fat-side down in a small, ovenproof skillet over low heat and let it cook until the fat is fully rendered, about 8 minutes. Flip the duck and transfer the skillet to the oven. Roast for 7 to 8 minutes or until it registers 145°F on an instant-read thermometer. Remove the skillet from the oven, let the duck cool and cut it into 16 equal-size slices.

NUOC CHAM SAUCE Whisk all the ingredients together in a medium bowl. Cover and refrigerate.

ASSEMBLY Wet a rice paper wrapper with hot water until just pliable. Lay it on a cutting board and add layers of carrot, cucumber and cabbage, 2 slices of duck, and then cilantro, basil and pickled onion. Roll tightly. Cover with a damp tea towel and repeat with the remaining wrappers and fillings.

Cut each roll into 7 equal pieces and serve with the nuoc cham sauce on the side.

CHEF'S NOTES

Always slice the duck as thinly as possible so cutting the rolls will be easy.

ROASTED PUMPKIN ROLL

Makes 56 pieces

ROASTED PUMPKIN

1½ pounds finely diced pumpkin

Extra-virgin olive oil

Salt

CHAI TEA VINAIGRETTE

2 cups rice wine vinegar

1 cinnamon stick

4 whole cloves

10 cardamom pods

2 star anise

1 teaspoon fennel seeds

2 teaspoons freshly ground black pepper

2 Darjeeling tea bags

2 (3 x 1-inch) strips of orange peel

½ garlic clove

0.1 ounce shallot, thinly sliced

¼ cup ice cubes

0.2 ounce salt

1½ cups neutral oil

8 sheets rice paper

Pickled Radishes (page 221)

4 ounces baby mustard greens

5.25 ounces grated carrot

1 cup toasted pepitas

½ cup chiffonade of fresh basil leaves

ROASTED PUMPKIN Preheat the oven to 350°F. On a large rimmed baking sheet, toss the pumpkin with extra-virgin olive oil and salt. Roast for 12 to 15 minutes or until tender. Remove from the oven and set aside to cool.

CHAI TEA VINAIGRETTE In a small saucepan, combine the rice wine vinegar, cinnamon, cloves, cardamom pods, star anise, fennel seeds and black pepper. Bring to a boil, reduce the heat to low and simmer until the sauce has reduced to ½ cup, about 15 minutes. Remove the pan from the heat and add the tea bags and orange peel. Steep for 3 minutes, then immediately strain the liquid through a fine-mesh sieve into a small bowl. Prepare an ice bath and set the bowl with the vinegar reduction in the water, being careful not to splash any water into the vinegar.

When the reduction has cooled, transfer it to a blender along with the garlic, shallot, ice and salt. Blend on high speed until smooth, then, with the motor running, slowly stream in the oil. Cover and refrigerate until needed.

ASSEMBLY Wet a rice paper wrapper with hot water until just pliable. Lay it on a cutting board and add layers of pumpkin, radish, mustard greens, carrot, pepitas and basil. Roll tightly. Cover with a damp tea towel and repeat with the remaining wrappers and fillings.

Cut each roll into 7 equal pieces and serve with the chai tea vinaigrette on the side.

KALE AND ROOT VEGETABLE ROLLS WITH CARROT-GINGER DIPPING SAUCE

Makes 56 pieces

CARROT-GINGER DIPPING SAUCE

8 ounces thinly sliced carrot

2 ounces ginger, peeled and smashed

1.5 ounces thinly sliced shallot

½ cup rice wine vinegar

1.5 ounces honey

¼ cup water

0.25 ounce salt

¾ cup extra-virgin olive oil

8 sheets rice paper

5.25 ounces chiffonade of lacinato kale

5.25 ounces julienned candy striped beets

Pickled Carrots (page 220)

5.25 ounces julienned English cucumber

1 cup fresh cilantro leaves

24 fresh mint leaves

CARROT-GINGER DIPPING SAUCE Combine all the ingredients except the extra-virgin olive oil in a blender. Blend on high speed until smooth, then, with the motor running, slowly stream in the oil. Cover and refrigerate until needed.

ASSEMBLY Wet a rice paper wrapper with hot water until just pliable. Lay it on a cutting board and add layers of kale, beets, pickled carrots, cucumber, cilantro and 3 mint leaves. Roll tightly. Cover with a damp tea towel and repeat with the remaining wrappers and fillings.

Cut each roll into 7 equal pieces and serve with the carrot-ginger sauce on the side.

EDUCATION IS EXPENSIVE

"Education is expensive." —Rena Gornitsky, grandmother

The learning curve for a twenty-something starting his own business is steep. All that glitters has not necessarily been gold. Yes, there have been triumphs. Too, there have been trials and a heavy dose of character-building experiences.

If you're wondering how to piss off your parents, I can tell you with exacting certainty that destroying a devoted home cook's range is a fast track to doing just that. My first year of business operations took place in my parents' house: the garage, my mom's beloved kitchen and every refrigerator and freezer I could get my hands on. I was taking over square foot by square foot, burner by burner, careening toward critical mass.

On a particularly busy weekend in 2007, I'd been cooking all day long. All of the burners were in constant use and I was prepping in the garage. Around 9 p.m. I heard a loud bang. I ran to the kitchen only to find that, due to the constant application of heat, the backsplash was coming crashing down, slab by slab. Needless to say, I began to look for kitchen space the next morning.

After an intense scouring of the commercial real estate market in Stamford, I opted to buy an 1,100-square-foot condo at $350 per foot void of any finishes or furnishings for empty warehouse space. After a steep purchase price, costly renovation and passing all facility inspections, OnTheMarc had a kitchen. This may've been the worst real estate deal in history, but I finally had a workspace to call my own.

In all of her wisdom, Rena was and continues to be spot-on.

SHISO WRAPS

Makes 50 pieces

SESAME VINAIGRETTE

1 ounce ginger, smashed

1 ounce garlic, smashed

5.5 ounces tahini

5 ounces rice wine vinegar

4 ounces water

1 ounce sesame oil

0.2 ounce salt

7 ounces extra-virgin olive oil

50 shiso leaves

4 to 5 ripe avocados, each cut into 14 slices

50 blood orange segments (from 5 to 6 oranges)

Salt

4 scallions, thinly sliced

½ cup toasted sesame seeds

SESAME VINAIGRETTE Combine all the ingredients except the extra-virgin olive oil in a blender. Blend on high speed until smooth, then, with the motor running, slowly stream in the oil. Transfer the vinaigrette to a squeeze bottle.

ASSEMBLY Lay the shiso leaves flat on a cutting board or work surface. Place a slice of avocado and an orange segment on each one, season with salt, and then sprinkle with scallions and sesame seeds. Give each piece a dot of sesame vinaigrette. Roll and serve immediately.

JAPANESE EGGPLANT PARMESAN

Makes 40 to 50 pieces

BRAISED EGGPLANT

4 or 5 (10-inch-long) Japanese eggplants

1 quart vegetable stock

4 garlic cloves, smashed

1 teaspoon whole black peppercorns

6 sprigs fresh thyme

TOASTED PANKO

1 tablespoon unsalted butter

1 cup panko breadcrumbs

2 teaspoons salt

2 cups Tomato Jam (page 215)

1 (8-ounce) ball fresh mozzarella cheese, cut into small dice

20 fresh basil leaves

BRAISED EGGPLANT Preheat the oven to 350°F.

Remove the top and bottom from the eggplants and then cut them in half lengthwise. Place them in a baking dish in one layer (use 2 pans if you need to) and pour in enough vegetable stock to come halfway up the sides of the eggplant pieces. Sprinkle the garlic, black pepper and thyme over the top.

Wrap the pans tightly with parchment paper and aluminum foil and braise them in the oven for 20 minutes.

Remove the eggplant from the oven and cut each piece into 1½-inch lengths. Set aside.

TOASTED PANKO Melt the butter in a sauté pan over medium heat. Add the panko and cook, tossing or stirring every minute or so, until it turns golden brown.

Remove the pan from the heat, season the panko with the salt and let it cool. Transfer to an airtight container and set aside until needed.

ASSEMBLY Preheat the oven to 350°F.

Arrange the eggplant pieces on large rimmed baking sheets in a single layer. On each piece, place one dollop of tomato jam and a cube or two of mozzarella. Heat in the oven for 3 to 4 minutes, then remove and garnish with the basil and a sprinkling of toasted panko. Serve immediately.

CHEF'S NOTES

You can flavor your breadcrumbs with anything! Some great options are crushed red pepper, lemon zest or dried oregano. Just remember to add these ingredients in the last 30 seconds of toasting so that they don't burn.

SAMOSA ROLLS

Makes 56 pieces

MINT YOGURT DIPPING SAUCE

2 cups plain, whole-fat Greek yogurt

2 tablespoons finely chopped fresh mint

¼ cup freshly squeezed lemon juice

0.3 ounce salt

POTATO FILLING

1½ pounds Yukon gold potatoes, finely diced

1 teaspoon ground coriander

1 teaspoon ground cardamom

1 teaspoon salt

1 tablespoon vegetable oil

FRIZZLED ONIONS

3 quarts vegetable oil, for frying

1 small (12-ounce) yellow onion, thinly sliced

1 cup cornstarch

8 sheets rice paper

4 ounces pickled ginger

6 ounces snow peas, cut into chiffonade

3 serrano chiles, seeded and finely sliced on a mandoline

MINT YOGURT DIPPING SAUCE In a medium bowl, whisk together all the ingredients. Cover and refrigerate until needed.

POTATO FILLING Preheat the oven to 350°F.

Spread the potatoes on a large, rimmed baking sheet and toss them with the coriander, cardamom, salt and oil. Roast for 12 to 15 minutes or until tender. Remove from the oven and set aside to cool.

FRIZZLED ONIONS Heat the oil in your deep fryer to 300°F.

In a large bowl, toss the onion with the cornstarch, then fry them for about 3 minutes or until light golden brown. Transfer to a paper towel-lined plate to drain.

ASSEMBLY Wet a rice paper wrapper with hot water until just pliable. Lay it on a cutting board and add layers of potato, pickled ginger, snow peas and frizzled onion. Roll tightly. Cover with a damp tea towel and repeat with the remaining wrappers and fillings.

Cut each roll into 7 equal pieces and garnish with a thin slice of serrano chile. Serve with the mint yogurt sauce on the side.

CHEF'S NOTES

Buy your pickled ginger at the sushi counter at your grocery store. It saves time and those sushi chefs have a secret recipe they definitely haven't shared.

SPECIAL TOOLS: Deep Fryer, Mandoline

THINK INSIDE THE CSA BOX

My wife and I are avid attendees of the Westport farmers' market. Admittedly, I am usually already at work by the time it opens, but on the occasion I am not, it's my favorite thing to do on Thursday mornings. E gets to go more often and my son, Ethan, loves it too.

Farmers' markets are so educational. Which farm has the first crop of cherry tomatoes? Who had the longest berry harvest? Where can I find the tastiest kale? It's all fantastic—learning about how to cook great things with seasonal ingredients—and how fleeting and special some of these ingredients can be.

In an age where you can source pomegranates any time of the year, or order an endless amount of summer squash in February, nothing is more refreshing than a farmers' market. It's essential to staying grounded as a chef. Seasonal cooking encourages a special, intense kind of creativity: certainly more challenging but also more rewarding. When in doubt, I always fall back on the old adage: "What grows together goes together."

VEGAN NORI ROLLS

Makes 40 to 50 pieces

HONEY-SESAME SAUCE

½ cup soy sauce

½ cup rice vinegar

6 tablespoons honey

2 scallions, finely chopped

4 tablespoons sesame seeds, toasted

2 tablespoons toasted sesame oil

8 sheets nori paper

2 cups Hummus (page 213)

1 tablespoon smoked paprika, toasted

4 ounces baby cress

1½ avocados, halved and pitted, each half cut into 12 slices

1 cup shelled edamame

Pickled Beets (page 220)

HONEY-SESAME SAUCE In a small bowl, whisk together all the ingredients. Cover and refrigerate until needed.

ASSEMBLY Lay out a sheet of nori. Using a spatula, spread about ¼ cup of hummus on the sheet, leaving a 1-inch strip at the top. Sprinkle with paprika. Sprinkle some of the baby cress on. Put 4 slices of avocado in a line, slightly overlapping. Sprinkle on some edamame in a line of about 12 beans. Sprinkle on some pickled beets. Roll tightly and cut into 6 or 7 pieces. Wet the uncovered edge with some water if the roll won't close.

CHAPTER FOUR

EXECUTION

One of the pillars OnTheMarc has been built on is the
idea that we prepare and cook everything on-site. When
describing our company and what we do, "full-service" doesn't
do it justice. I like to explain to people that we are a lot like a
roving restaurant: we bring the entire staff, we build a kitchen
each time and, of course, we bring the food and drinks.

In the interest of providing our clients with the
best possible end product, the majority of our food
preparation and cooking happens at the event. One of the
ways I achieve this is by hiring restaurant chefs who have
never worked in catering before. People are generally
surprised to hear this, given the notion that caterers just
bring everything in pans and heat them on-site.

Does cooking on-site present challenges? Of course.
We spend time flipping breakers, strategizing our kitchen
location and worrying about power sources. Most importantly,
all of our food is fired like it would be in a restaurant:
à la minute and served to our clients immediately.

MIXED TEMPURA: AVOCADO, SHISHITO PEPPERS AND PRESERVED LEMONS

Makes 40 to 50 pieces

PRESERVED LEMONS

2 lemons

2 tablespoons kosher salt

2 tablespoons sugar

1 teaspoon mustard seeds, toasted

¼ teaspoon fennel seeds

1 bay leaf

¼ cup water

BLACK PEPPER CREMA

1 cup sour cream

1 cup heavy cream

1 teaspoon salt

1 tablespoon coarsely ground black pepper

TEMPURA BATTER

Double recipe Dry Tempura Mix (page 224)

4½ cups water

3 quarts vegetable oil, for frying

4 ripe avocados, halved, pits removed

20 shishito peppers

Salt

PRESERVED LEMONS Bring 2 quarts of water to a boil in a large pot.

Slice the lemons thinly (1⁄16 inch thick) on a mandoline. You will have more slices than you need.

Blanch the lemons in the boiling water for 30 seconds, then immediately drain them in a colander and set them aside to cool. When they have reached room temperature, place them in a resealable plastic bag.

Meanwhile, in a small saucepan, combine the salt, sugar, mustard, fennel, bay leaf and water and cook over low heat until the sugar and salt are dissolved.

Remove the pan from the heat and let the pickling liquid cool, then pour it into the bag with the lemons. Seal the bag, making sure to suck out as much air as possible so that the lemons are fully submerged in the liquid. Lay the bag flat in the refrigerator. The lemons should be ready in 3 to 4 days. Remove the lemons from the cure and rinse to prepare for the deep fryer.

BLACK PEPPER CREMA Combine all the ingredients in an airtight container, cover and allow to sit for 3 hours at room temperature. This can be done right before your party starts.

TEMPURA BATTER In a large bowl, whisk together the tempura mix and water. Set aside.

ASSEMBLY Heat the vegetable oil in your deep fryer to 350°F.

Using a paring knife, make 2 lengthwise cuts and one widthwise cut in each avocado half, so that you have 6 roughly equal-size pieces. Leave the avocados in their shell until ready to use.

Using tongs, chopsticks or kitchen tweezers, dip the avocado pieces, peppers and lemon slices in the tempura batter, shaking off the excess.

Drop the battered vegetables into the fryer one at a time. The vegetables will take 30 seconds to 1 minute to fry, depending on how big they are.

Remove the tempura from the fryer, season with salt and serve warm with the black pepper crema on the side.

CHEF'S NOTES

PRO TIP: The avocado halves can be put back together and wrapped in plastic or lightly coated with cooking spray to prevent browning.

SPECIAL TOOLS: Deep Fryer, Mandoline

FRITTO MISTO

Makes 40 to 50 pieces

2 pounds calamari, cleaned and trimmed

4 cups buttermilk, divided

2 cups coarsely ground cornmeal

2 cups all-purpose flour

1 ounce Old Bay Seasoning

1 (16-ounce) jar pepperoncini

1 (15.75-ounce) jar caper berries

SQUID INK AIOLI

2 cups Homemade Mayonnaise (page 214)

4 teaspoons squid ink

1 tablespoon freshly squeezed lemon juice

3 quarts vegetable oil, for frying

Salt

4 scallions, thinly sliced

4 tablespoons freshly grated lemon zest

Rinse the calamari and shake dry. In a large bowl, submerge the calamari in 2 cups of the buttermilk for a few seconds, just to coat, then drain.

In a separate bowl, whisk together the cornmeal, flour and Old Bay Seasoning. Drain the calamari and toss it in the breading mixture, then transfer the breaded calamari to a wire rack.

In a large bowl, submerge the pepperoncini and caper berries in the remaining 2 cups of buttermilk for a few seconds. Drain, toss in the remaining breading mixture and transfer to the wire rack with the calamari.

SQUID INK AIOLI In a bowl, whisk together the mayonnaise, squid ink and lemon juice until well combined. Cover and refrigerate until ready to use.

ASSEMBLY Heat the oil in your deep fryer to 350°F.

Drop a handful of capers and pepperoncini into the fryer, wait 2 minutes and then add a handful of calamari. Fry for 30 seconds longer; immediately remove the vegetables and calamari to a paper towel-lined plate and season with salt, scallions and lemon zest. Repeat with the remaining capers, pepperoncini and calamari.

Serve immediately with the squid ink aioli on the side.

CHEF'S NOTES

SPECIAL TOOLS: Deep Fryer

MINI CORN DOGS

The adult request for little hot dogs is, as you may not be aware, at an all-time high. In my ten years of catering experience, there is one thing that holds true: people like what they like. And people like pigs in a blanket.

It doesn't matter whether the event is upscale, casual, corporate or for kids. We've yet to meet a guest who doesn't, at the very least, smile when offered a tray of mini corn dogs. Sure, we'll serve you little hot dogs on baby brioche buns if you want, but mini corn dogs are our idea of a good time.

This miniature version of a classic is conceptually playful—and we're sure to present it playfully, too. Serve these with our OnTheMarc Signature Ketchup (page 214) and/or spicy brown mustard straight from the jar.

Makes 50 pieces

25 Kobe or high-quality cocktail franks

CORN DOG BATTER

1 cup coarsely ground cornmeal

½ teaspoon kosher salt

2 cups all-purpose flour

1½ teaspoons baking powder

3¾ tablespoons sugar

3 cups whole milk

3 quarts vegetable oil, for frying

Salt

2 cups spicy brown mustard

Cut all the cocktail franks in half on an extreme bias and skewer them through the cut sides. Place the skewered franks on a platter; cover and refrigerate.

CORN DOG BATTER In a large bowl, whisk together all of the batter ingredients until smooth.

ASSEMBLY Heat the oil in your deep fryer to 350°F.

Dip a skewered frank in the corn dog batter, shake off any excess and drop into the fryer a few at a time. Fry for 1½ to 2 minutes or until the batter is crisp and golden brown, then immediately remove the corn dogs to a paper towel-lined plate and season with salt. Repeat with the remaining franks.

Serve immediately with the mustard on the side.

CHEF'S NOTES

SPECIAL TOOLS: Deep Fryer, 50 Skewers

CHICKEN FRITES WITH FORMULA 313 DIPPING SAUCE

Makes 40 to 50 frites

FORMULA 313 DIPPING SAUCE

2 cups oyster sauce

2 cups rice wine vinegar

7 tablespoons sriracha

1 cup sugar

3 tablespoons sesame oil

1 tablespoon freshly ground black pepper

CHICKEN FRITES

3 pounds boneless, skinless chicken breasts

Salt

2 cups all-purpose flour

12 large eggs, beaten

4 cups panko breadcrumbs

3 quarts vegetable oil, for frying

Salt

FORMULA 313 DIPPING SAUCE Combine all the ingredients in a bowl and whisk thoroughly. Transfer to an airtight container and refrigerate until ready to use.

CHICKEN FRITES Remove any fat or gristle from the chicken breasts. Cut the chicken into ½-inch by 1½-inch strips, place them in an airtight container and season with about 1 ounce of salt. Cover and refrigerate for a few hours.

When you're ready to bread the chicken, drain it of any excess liquid and pat it dry. Put your flour, eggs and panko into three separate containers.

Toss each strip of chicken in the flour, shake off any excess, and then dip it in the egg. Let the excess egg drip off, and finally coat the chicken in the panko. Place the breaded chicken piece on a parchment-lined baking sheet and repeat with the remaining chicken and breading components.

ASSEMBLY Heat the oil in your deep fryer to 350°F.

Working in batches, fry the breaded chicken pieces for 2 to 3 minutes, until cooked through and golden brown. Remove them to a paper towel-lined plate and season with salt.

Serve the frites immediately with the dipping sauce on the side.

___

CHEF'S NOTES

What's Formula 313, you ask? Formula 313, named for the day Erica and I met, is a signature OTM sauce with a cult following. We make it in house and serve it with a variety of hors d'oeuvres, including the chicken frites. It's love at first bite.

SPECIAL TOOLS: Deep Fryer

PEKING DUCK PANCAKES

Long before I learned to cook duck breast at the CIA, I went to Chinatown to eat Peking duck with my family. At Peking Duck House, my parents taught my brother and I the art of layering: delicate pancake, hoisin sauce, duck meat, scallion, cucumber and finally, crispy skin. It remains to this day one of my favorite things to eat. While cooking true Peking duck requires several days of work, you can get nearly the same payoff with this seared duck breast. For the best results, make your pancakes right before you serve them.

Makes 40 to 50 pieces

DUCK BREAST

2 magret duck breasts (about 1 pound total)

2 teaspoons vegetable oil

GLUTEN-FREE PANCAKES (MAKES 75 PANCAKES)

2.65 ounces rice flour

1.35 ounces garbanzo flour

1.35 ounces cornmeal

0.9 ounce sugar

0.25 ounce baking powder

0.07 ounce kosher salt

2 large eggs

1 cup whole milk

2 tablespoons duck fat or vegetable oil

3 Persian cucumbers, sliced into ⅛-inch-thick rounds

1 (8-ounce) jar hoisin sauce

4 scallions, thinly sliced

DUCK BREAST Score the skin of each duck breast in a crosshatch pattern, making sure that you do not cut all the way through the skin. (Halfway in is enough for it to render properly.)

Add the vegetable oil to a medium sauté pan and place the duck breasts on top, skin-side down. Place the pan over very low heat and allow the duck to sear slowly, shaking the pan every minute or so to prevent the duck from sticking to the bottom, and draining the duck fat a few times as needed. The goal is to cook all the fat out of the skin so that all you have left is crispy, crunchy skin and no chewy fat. This process will take about 8 minutes total. Make sure you save 2 tablespoons of the duck fat for making the pancakes.

When the skin is fully rendered, remove the duck breasts from the pan and set them aside to cool.

Preheat the oven to 350°F.

About 15 minutes before you want to make this appetizer, finish the duck breasts in the oven for about 4 minutes for medium doneness.

Remove the duck from the oven and allow it to rest for 2 or 3 minutes, then cut each breast in half lengthwise and cut each half into ⅛-inch-thick slices. Tent the duck with foil to keep it warm.

CONTINUED >

GLUTEN-FREE PANCAKES Preheat a griddle over medium heat, or to 350°F.

Mix all the dry ingredients in a medium bowl.

In separate bowl, mix together the wet ingredients. Add the wet ingredients to the dry ingredients and whisk thoroughly to incorporate.

Grease the griddle with the duck fat or vegetable oil and spoon quarter-size dollops of batter onto it, spacing them ½ inch apart.

Cook the pancakes for about 45 seconds on the first side, flip and cook for 15 more seconds or until golden brown and springy to the touch.

Repeat with the remaining batter. Cover and keep warm.

ASSEMBLY Preheat the oven to 350°F.

Place some of the pancakes on a baking sheet and warm them in the oven for 90 seconds.

Remove from the oven and put one slice of cucumber, one slice of duck, a dab of hoisin and a couple pieces of scallion on top of each warmed pancake.

Serve immediately.

CHEF'S NOTES

Use Bob's Red Mill gluten-free pancake mix to save time.

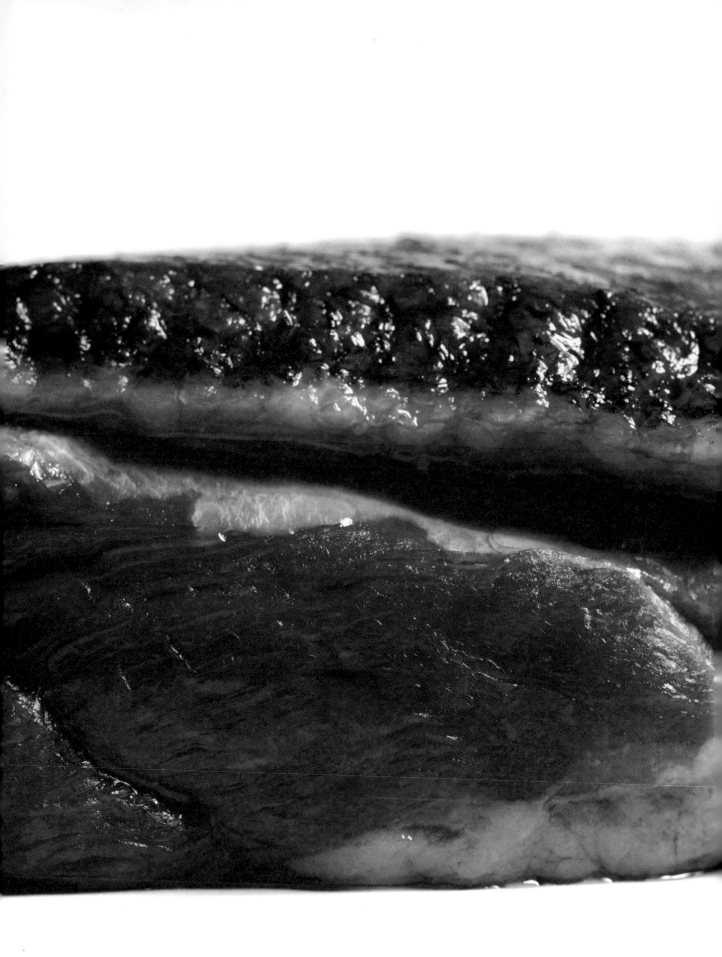

SESAME CHICKEN ON MISO TUILES

For a few weeks, every time I walked into the OTM kitchen following a "try this!" call from Amos, my executive chef, I was met with a miso-something. Though the miso pound cake didn't make the final cut, these delicate wafers were an instant hit. We matched their savory flavor with brined and grilled chicken, fresh edamame and sesame dressing. The tuiles themselves are a little tough to nail down: they have to be thick enough not to crack under the toppings, but thin enough to remain crispy.

Makes 40 to 50 pieces

3 pounds boneless, skinless chicken thighs

2 quarts Poultry Brine (page 215)

SESAME VINAIGRETTE

1 ounce fresh ginger, smashed

1 ounce garlic, smashed

5.5 ounces tahini

5 ounces rice wine vinegar

4 ounces water

1 ounce sesame oil

0.2 ounce salt

7 ounces extra-virgin olive oil

Salt

40 to 50 Tuiles (page 216)

4 scallions, thinly sliced

½ cup shelled edamame, cooked

1 cup sesame seeds, toasted

Clean the chicken of any fat and gristle and place in a deep container.

Allow the brine to cool to room temperature, then pour it over the chicken. Cover and refrigerate for at least 4 hours, preferably overnight if possible. Drain and pat the chicken dry.

Preheat one side of a two-zone grill to high heat, and the other side to low. Grill the chicken over high heat for 3 minutes per side, then finish it on the cooler side for another 5 minutes.

Immediately remove the chicken from the grill and set it aside. When it has cooled completely, slice the chicken as thinly as possible, place it in an airtight container and store in the refrigerator until needed.

SESAME VINAIGRETTE Add everything except the olive oil to a blender. Process until smooth, then, with the motor running on high, slowly drizzle in the oil. Refrigerate the vinaigrette in an airtight container until needed.

ASSEMBLY Mix the sliced chicken with ¼ cup of the sesame vinaigrette and season with salt to taste. Both the vinaigrette and the chicken are already seasoned, so take care not to overseason the chicken salad.

Place a heaping tablespoon of chicken salad on a tuile and garnish with the scallions, edamame and sesame seeds.

Serve immediately.

FAMOUS LAST WORDS

Grilling: an unusual cooking method for chocolate lava cakes, I know, but successful in times of difficulty. There are challenges you can prepare for and those you simply can't predict. Here's one of the more colorful ways I found out.

A few years after the inception of OnTheMarc, we had an event much like the others: a dinner party at a private residence. The menu consisted of OTM favorites and the clients were regulars. I had my A team with me and we were ready to knock it out of the park. The only difference was that the weather was apocalyptic—showers of rain became sheets, sheets became waterfalls. The stormy weather was unrelenting and only worsened over the course of the night.

"No sweat—we're cooking inside." Famous last words.

Before we could even make it to serving the main course, the house next door was hit by lighting, caught on fire, and caused the power to go out for the entire area—including our venue for the evening. We could pull off the remainder of the savory food by stovetop and candlelight, sure, but what about dessert? The ovens were out of commission and it was a baked item. The only answer was the grill.

Turns out going outside, into the storm, was the solution. With an umbrella in one hand and raw lava cakes in the other, I fired up the grill and set the cakes to work. I don't remember being nervous and I neverdoubted our ability to put the food out. My prevailing memory is loving the challenge. The guests loved the chocolate cakes, too.

It's on these days, despite the odds, that we are actually doing our best work. We anticipate as much as we can but accept a certain level of unpredictability with open arms. And we are wiser for it.

CHICKEN AND WAFFLES

Makes 40 to 50 pieces

1 recipe Chicken Frites (page 72)

WAFFLES

1 large egg

¾ cup plus 2 tablespoons buttermilk

4 tablespoons unsalted butter, melted

1 teaspoon vanilla extract

1 cup pastry flour

1 tablespoon sugar

1 teaspoon baking powder

½ teaspoon baking soda

½ teaspoon kosher salt

3 quarts vegetable oil, for frying

¾ cup (1½ sticks) unsalted butter, for brushing

Salt

1 cup Vermont pure maple syrup, grade A

1 ounce chive sprouts, minced

CHICKEN FRITES Trim, cut and bread the chicken as described on page 72, and reserve the breaded chicken pieces on a parchment-lined baking sheet. This step can be done a few days ahead, and the chicken can be frozen until ready to use.

WAFFLES Preheat your waffle iron.

In a large bowl, whisk together the egg, buttermilk, melted butter and vanilla.

Combine the dry ingredients in a separate, large bowl and mix thoroughly. Add the wet ingredients to the dry ingredients and mix well until there are only a few lumps remaining in the batter.

Spray the waffle iron with cooking spray and pour in about ⅓ cup of the batter. Close the iron and remove the waffle when it stops steaming, after about 3 minutes.

Repeat with the remaining batter and set the cooked waffles on a wire rack to cool.

When ready, cut the waffles into individual "cups."

If you don't plan to assemble the chicken and waffles right away, wrap the waffles in foil and refrigerate or freeze until needed.

CONTINUED >

ASSEMBLY Preheat the oven and heat the oil in your deep fryer to 350°F.

Melt the butter in a small saucepan over low heat, cover and keep warm.

Drop a few chicken frites into the fryer and cook until golden brown, 2 to 3 minutes. Immediately remove the frites to a paper towel-lined plate and season with salt. Repeat with the remaining chicken.

While the chicken is frying, brush a few waffle pieces with the melted butter, place them on a baking sheet and heat in the oven for 3 minutes. Remove the waffles from the oven.

Chop the chicken into small pieces so it fits in the nooks of the waffles.

Drizzle the chicken and waffles with maple syrup and sprinkle with chives.

Serve immediately.

CHEF'S NOTES

Buckwheat waffles can be made by substituting the pastry flour for buckwheat flour in even amounts.

SPECIAL TOOLS: Deep Fryer, Squeeze Bottle (for the maple syrup), Paintbrush (for buttering the waffles), Waffle Iron

CHICKEN-FRIED SWEETBREAD BISCUITS

Though sweetbreads might be a little bit intimidating to prepare at first, this is one of the most approachable ways to eat them. Once fried, serve immediately.

Makes 40 to 50 pieces

SWEETBREADS

5 pounds sweetbreads

2 lemons, cut in half

1 bay leaf

3 ounces white wine vinegar

4 cups buttermilk

4 cups all-purpose flour

2 quarts vegetable oil, for frying

Salt and freshly ground black pepper

BISCUITS

2 cups all-purpose flour

1½ tablespoons baking powder

1 teaspoon salt

1 tablespoon sugar

2 cups heavy cream, divided

Black Pepper Gravy (page 213)

SWEETBREADS Rinse the sweetbreads in cold water. Place in a large pot and cover with water by 2 inches with the lemons, bay leaf and vinegar. Bring to a boil, shut off, strain and shock the sweetbreads in an ice bath.

Transfer to a tea towel and wring out. Remove any gristle or sinew and lay on a towel to dry for 5 minutes. Cut into 1½-inch pieces and toss with the buttermilk in a bowl. A few pieces at a time, toss the sweetbreads in the flour; shake off excess flour and lay on a clean baking sheet lined with parchment.

Preheat the oven to 375°F. Heat the oil in your deep fryer to 350°F.

BISCUITS Whisk all the dry ingredients together in a bowl. Using a wooden spoon, fold the flour while streaming in 1½ cups of heavy cream. The dough should look shaggy and messy. Do not mix past this stage. Use a spoon and scoop balls about 2 tablespoons in size onto a parchment-lined sheet pan. Brush the remaining ½ cup heavy cream onto the biscuits. Bake for 5 to 6 minutes or until golden brown at the edges.

While the biscuits are baking, fry the sweetbreads, a handful at a time, for 2 to 3 minutes or until golden brown. Remove to a plate lined with paper towels and season with salt and pepper. Cut all cooled biscuits in half like a sandwich. Put a nugget of sweetbreads inside each one.

To serve, reheat in a 350°F oven for 2 to 3 minutes until just warm. Top with a tablespoon of black pepper gravy and serve immediately.

CHAPTER FIVE

BUILDING ON CLASSICS

Pizza, especially in the Northeast, is well loved. Everyone has their simple, feel-good order: margherita, a regular slice, half pepperoni, half cheese..."Pizza Night" was something most of my friends and family celebrated at least once a week growing up (something I acutely understand now that I have become a busy parent myself).

When I first began catering, I had a fear of dough. I avoided using yeast at all costs and baked only when necessary. But then I went to Italy. Erica and I traveled all over, and while the other dishes were also awesome, it was the pizzas, piadine and flatbreads that really stayed with me.

My executive chef Amos has always loved working with bread dough and he's not afraid of a challenge. When I returned from my trip, I went straight to him with my stories of magical, delicious pizzas and flatbreads. We decided that events at OnTheMarc needed flatbreads. So, with a little inspiration and a lot of experimentation, we sought out the best way to serve pizza in a catered setting (a setting that is largely different each time.) We were pleased to discover that grilling the dough had a mouthwatering effect. Plus, the request for pizza is, as you can imagine, very frequent.

SPICY CALABRESE FLATBREADS

The Italians who first inspired our foray into flatbreads might shake their heads at this one—a combination of tangy tomato molasses, roasted red onion, spicy Calabrese salami, pickled blueberries and creamy mascarpone—but we aren't afraid to be different.

Makes 36 to 48 pieces

TOMATO MOLASSES REDUCTION

2 pounds Roma tomatoes, juiced

3 ounces honey

6 ounces champagne vinegar

1.5 ounces molasses

ROASTED RED ONIONS

1 large red onion, thinly sliced

2 tablespoons extra-virgin olive oil

Salt and freshly ground black pepper

1 (16-ounce) tub mascarpone cheese

6 Flatbreads (page 217)

Salt and freshly ground black pepper

Pickled Blueberries (page 220)

1 (4- to 6-inch) spicy Calabrese salami, sliced as thinly as possible

TOMATO MOLASSES REDUCTION Combine all the ingredients in a medium saucepan over medium-high heat. Bring the mixture to a boil and cook uncovered for 16 minutes or until it coats the back of a spoon and holds the line when you drag your finger through it.

Fill a large bowl halfway with ice water. Once the sauce has reduced, immediately remove the pan from the heat and set the pan in the bowl of ice water, being careful not to splash any water into the sauce. When the sauce is cool, transfer it to an airtight container and refrigerate until needed.

ROASTED RED ONIONS Preheat the oven to 450°F.

In a medium bowl, toss the onion with the olive oil, salt and pepper, then spread it out on a rimmed baking sheet. Roast for 10 minutes or until the onions begin to char at the ends.

Remove the baking sheet from the oven and set the onions aside to cool.

ASSEMBLY Reduce the oven temperature to 350°F.

Smear a thick layer of mascarpone cheese on each flatbread piece, sprinkle with salt and pepper, and garnish with the roasted onions. Place the flatbreads on large baking sheets and reheat in the oven for 5 minutes.

Remove the flatbreads from the oven and garnish with the blueberries and spicy salami, finishing with a good drizzle of tomato molasses.

Cut each flatbread into 6 to 8 equal-size pieces.

Serve immediately.

CHEF'S NOTES

All of these components should be done the day before your party; the flatbreads can be made the day of.

When putting the ingredients on your pizza, the goal is to have a bit of every ingredient in every bite, so garnish accordingly.

SPECIAL TOOLS: A plastic squeeze bottle for the tomato molasses will make drizzling easier and help lend a pro/artistic touch to the garnishing part.

GRILLED CHICKEN FLATBREADS

Makes 36 to 48 pieces

CHICKEN

1 pound boneless, skinless chicken thighs

½ gallon Poultry Brine (page 215)

RICOTTA

2 cups whole milk

1 cup heavy cream

0.25 ounce kosher salt

¼ cup white distilled vinegar

GARLIC CHIPS

3 ounces garlic cloves, peeled

Vegetable oil, as needed

CURED EGG YOLKS

1¾ cups kosher salt

1¼ cups sugar

4 egg yolks

6 Flatbreads (page 217)

Salt and freshly ground pepper

1 (1-pound) ball smoked mozzarella, roughly torn into bite-size pieces

Leaves from 1 bunch fresh oregano

Extra-virgin olive oil, as needed

CHICKEN Place the chicken in a deep, airtight container and pour the brine over; seal and refrigerate for 8 hours or overnight.

Preheat the grill to high and preheat the oven to 350°F. Grill the chicken thighs for 2 minutes per side, then finish in the oven until fully cooked. Let them rest for 5 minutes. Slice them as thinly as possible and set aside.

RICOTTA Combine the milk, cream and salt in a medium saucepan fitted with a candy thermometer and bring the mixture to 195°F over medium-high heat.

As soon as the temperature is reached, remove the pan from the heat and sprinkle with the vinegar; you will see the curds and whey separate.

Line a colander with cheesecloth and set it over a large bowl. Pour the ricotta into the prepared colander and strain the ricotta in the fridge overnight.

GARLIC CHIPS Using a mandoline, slice the garlic as thinly as you can.

Place the slices in a small saucepan and pour in enough vegetable oil to cover them completely. Place the pan over low heat and let the garlic cook very slowly.

Once the garlic turns a light golden brown, use a slotted spoon to remove it to a paper towel-lined plate. The chips will crisp up as they sit.

CURED EGG YOLKS In a wide, shallow, airtight plastic container, whisk together the salt and sugar. Scoop one-third of this mixture into another bowl and set aside.

Level the salt/sugar mixture in the first bowl into an even layer and use the back of a spoon to make 4 evenly spaced depressions.

CONTINUED >

Gently lay an egg yolk in each depression and use the reserved salt/sugar mixture to fully cover the tops so that the yolks are buried in the cure.

Seal the container and refrigerate for 4 days.

After 4 days have passed, gently remove the yolks and brush off all of the salt/sugar mixture.

Preheat the oven to 150°F. Place the cured yolks on a wire rack set inside a rimmed baking sheet and dehydrate in the oven for 1½ to 2 hours or overnight with the oven light on. They should be firm and no longer tacky on the surface.

Store the cured egg yolks in an airtight container at room temperature until needed.

ASSEMBLY Preheat the oven to 350°F.

Smear a thick layer of ricotta on each flatbread piece, and sprinkle with salt and pepper. Next, add some sliced chicken and some of the smoked mozzarella. Place the flatbread pieces on large baking sheets and heat them for 5 minutes in the oven.

Remove the flatbreads from the oven and garnish with the garlic chips, oregano and a drizzle of extra-virgin olive oil. Using a microplane, grate a healthy amount of cured egg yolk over the top of each flatbread.

Cut each flatbread into 6 to 8 equal-size pieces.

Serve immediately.

CHEF'S NOTES

The leftover oil from the garlic chips is way tasty. Use it for making salad dressings, sautéing meat or toasting grains.

SPECIAL TOOLS: Mandoline, Microplane, Cheesecloth

POMEGRANATE AND GOAT CHEESE FLATBREADS

Makes 36 to 48 pieces

WHIPPED GOAT CHEESE

9 ounces fresh goat cheese

9 ounces heavy cream

0.1 ounce kosher salt

0.05 ounce freshly ground black pepper

PORT WINE REDUCTION

4 cups port wine

1 cup white balsamic vinegar

4 ounces sugar

GRILLED SCALLIONS

4 bunches scallions

Olive oil

Salt and freshly ground pepper

6 Flatbreads (page 217)

Salt and freshly ground black pepper

2 cups pomegranate seeds

Extra-virgin olive oil, for drizzling

WHIPPED GOAT CHEESE In the bowl of a stand mixer fitted with the whisk attachment, whip the goat cheese on high speed until it crumbles.

Continue mixing until it comes back together. As the goat cheese begins to fluff up a little, start drizzling in the heavy cream in a constant stream until none is left.

When the last of the cream is incorporated, turn off the mixer and add the salt and pepper. Whisk a few times to incorporate the spices, then transfer the goat cheese mixture to an airtight container.

PORT WINE REDUCTION Combine all the ingredients in a medium saucepan over medium-high heat. Bring the mixture to a boil and cook uncovered for 16 minutes or until it reaches the consistency of dark amber maple syrup.

Fill a large bowl halfway with ice water. Once the sauce has reduced, immediately remove the pan from the heat and set the pan in the bowl of ice water, being careful not to splash any water into the sauce. When the sauce is cool, transfer it to an airtight container and set it aside at room temperature until needed.

CONTINUED >

GRILLED SCALLIONS Preheat a grill to high. Toss the scallions with the olive oil, salt and pepper and grill them for about 2 minutes per side, or until slightly charred and just wilted. Remove them from the grill and set aside.

ASSEMBLY Preheat the oven to 350°F.

Smear a thick layer of whipped goat cheese on each flatbread piece and season with salt and pepper, then scatter on some grilled scallions. Place the flatbreads on large baking sheets and heat in the oven for 5 minutes.

Remove the flatbreads from the oven and top them with the pomegranate seeds, a drizzle of extra-virgin olive oil and some port wine reduction.

Cut each flatbread into 6 to 8 equal-size pieces.

Serve immediately.

CHEF'S NOTES

When making the whipped goat cheese, make sure everything is very cold; you can even refrigerate the bowl for 30 minutes.

CLAM AND BACON FLATBREADS

Surf and turf in an old-school, clams casino kind of way, this flatbread pairs briny clams with smoky bacon in a slight departure from New Haven's beloved clam pizza. Pepe's on Wooster Street in New Haven, Connecticut, is one of the most famous pizza places in the world, and their most famous pie is the White Clam Pizza. Local inspiration is very frequently the basis for client requests, and we are more than happy to oblige. Our clam and bacon flatbread came to us just this way. You're welcome to cook clams for this, but it's just as good with those cooked by your local fish guy.

Makes 36 to 48 pieces

POTATO BÉCHAMEL

1 tablespoon unsalted butter

4 ounces minced yellow onion

2 garlic cloves, minced

1 ounce all-purpose flour

1 quart whole milk

Pinch of freshly ground black pepper

Pinch of freshly ground nutmeg

2 ounces potato flakes

0.25 ounce kosher salt

8 ounces thick-cut bacon, sliced

6 Flatbreads (page 217)

Salt and freshly ground black pepper

8 ounces cooked and cleaned littleneck clams (bought from the seafood section at the market)

Leaves from 1 bunch fresh thyme

Extra-virgin olive oil

POTATO BÉCHAMEL Melt the butter in a medium saucepan over medium heat. Add the onion and sauté for 2 to 3 minutes or until soft and translucent. Add the garlic and sauté for 30 seconds, just until fragrant.

Sprinkle the flour over the onion and garlic and cook for 2 minutes, stirring constantly so the roux does not burn or stick to the bottom of the pan.

Slowly whisk the milk into the roux, 1 cup at a time, making sure the mixture is completely smooth before adding the next cup.

Bring the mixture just to a boil while stirring constantly; remove the pan from the heat and whisk in the pepper, nutmeg, potato flakes and salt.

Cover and keep warm on the stovetop until needed.

Cut the bacon into lardons or fat matchsticks and fry them in a large skillet over low heat until just crisp.

Remove the bacon to a paper towel-lined plate and set aside.

ASSEMBLY Preheat the oven to 350°F.

Smear a thick layer of potato béchamel on each flatbread piece, sprinkle with salt and pepper and lay a few clams on top. Place the flatbreads on large baking sheets and heat them in the oven for 5 minutes.

Remove the flatbreads from the oven and scatter on the bacon and thyme, finishing with a drizzle of extra-virgin olive oil.

Cut each flatbread into 6 to 8 equal-size pieces.

Serve immediately.

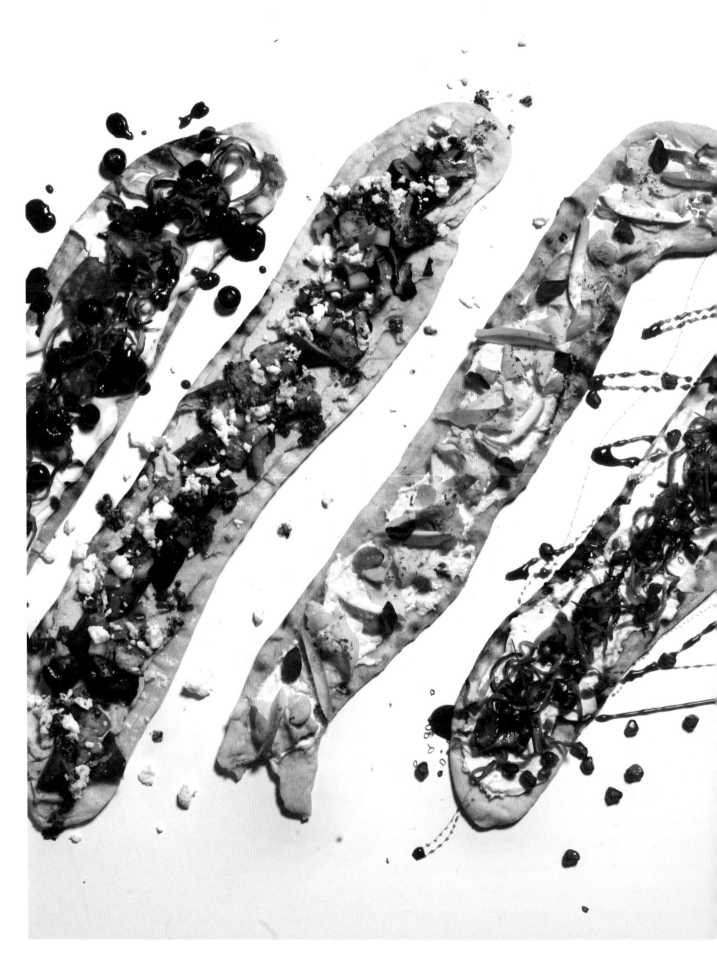

CLASSIC FOR A REASON

When OnTheMarc became the exclusive catering partner at The Inn at Longshore in 2015, I was tapped to update the food and wine program at a classic, well-loved venue. The challenge was straightforward but intense: walk into an established business and breathe new life into it.

Classics are "classic" for a reason—their cornerstones are unchanging, and they only require new life and energy. Like a classic car may be a benchmark for future models in the auto industry, "The Inn" is a nod to the quaint East Coast, and people have an enduring appreciation for that.

The appreciation for a quintessential, charming New England experience needs an equally charming and classic dining experience with contemporary sensibilities. After the first transitional year full of collaboration, tough decisions and upgrades, my first on-premise exclusive venue was truly born.

The learning curve in terms of on-premise catering was steep. It taught me a lot about patience. Putting positive change into effect on a large scale takes time and tons of energy. My goal was always to listen first and act second. I asked myself, my team and my mentors: What's working? What could be better? And most importantly, who is our audience?

My style of food has always maintained an honest simplicity, but it's unique and interesting. I am used to people asking me to make creative menus for them. This, however, was atypical to the clients at Longshore. Many have a clear idea (before coming in) of what they would like to eat and when, down to the butter with the bread. It was a challenge I had yet to face and it is now, along with my other exclusive venues, an evolving work in progress.

HUMMUS AND CHARRED EGGPLANT FLATBREADS

Makes 40 to 50 pieces

PICKLED PERSIMMONS

8 ounces ripe persimmons

2 cups Pickling Liquid, made with the addition of 15 cardamom pods (page 219)

CHARRED EGGPLANT

4 Japanese eggplants

Extra-virgin olive oil

Salt

PARSLEY SALSA VERDE (MAKES 1 CUP)

½ cup olive oil, divided

4 garlic cloves, minced

1 tablespoon lemon zest

3 cups flat-leaf parsley leaves, finely chopped

Salt and pepper to taste

2 cups Hummus (page 213)

6 Flatbreads (page 217)

1½ cups crumbled feta cheese

PICKLED PERSIMMONS Pack the persimmons into a large canning jar or other heatproof container with a lid. Make the pickling liquid. When it comes to a boil, strain the liquid through a fine-mesh sieve into the jar with the persimmons. Let cool to room temperature, then seal the jar and refrigerate overnight.

The next day, drain the persimmons and dice them into small pieces.

CHARRED EGGPLANT Preheat a grill to high. In a large bowl, toss the eggplants with extra-virgin olive oil and grill them until cooked through and charred on all sides, 8 to 10 minutes. Remove the stems, chop coarsely, season with salt and transfer to an airtight container. Refrigerate until needed.

PARSLEY SALSA VERDE Mix ¼ cup of the olive oil with the garlic and lemon zest and let stand for 20 minutes. Add the parsley and stir until well coated. Add the remaining ¼ cup oil and season to taste. Set aside.

ASSEMBLY Preheat the oven to 350°F.

Spread a layer of hummus on each flatbread piece and scatter on some charred eggplant. Place the flatbreads on large baking sheets and heat in the oven for 5 minutes.

Remove the flatbreads from the oven and garnish with the persimmons, feta and a drizzle of salsa verde.

Cut into bite-size pieces and serve immediately.

CHAPTER SIX

HONOR THE INGREDIENT

I was three weeks into my first cooking job and I had managed to screw up the crispy carrots every single night since I got there.

My shift started the same way, day in and day out: I'd go down a narrow staircase to the basement walk-in and get a huge amount of cleaned carrots.

I then peeled long carrot ribbons that would later be sprinkled with flour and fried for a garnish. Except that sprinkling and frying part proved to be hard. I couldn't grasp the concept, and I'd turn up a clumpy mess, repeatedly.

As I've matured as a chef I've come to understand that cooking is very much a science. Grasping the concept, for me, was the key to proper execution: the first time I got the crispy carrots right marked the day I stopped getting them wrong.

Thanks to infamous chefs like Charlie Trotter and my personal carrot saga, much of my cooking is inspired by variations on a single ingredient. We offer several ingredient-themed dishes, including heirloom carrots four ways, summer tomatoes three ways and so on. Fundamentally understanding the many expressions of a single ingredient has become one of the cornerstones of my style as a chef.

This chapter happens to highlight the potato: starchy, versatile and satisfying.

MICRO LATKES WITH CAVIAR AND CRÈME FRAÎCHE

It's not uncommon to see chefs upgrade their favorite childhood eats in elegant and interesting ways. The latke is such an iconic food central to Jewish celebrations—we ate them all the time growing up and I still love them today.

It wasn't until a trip to Seattle and a subsequent meal with my mom, however, that I was exposed to a more elegant version of one of my favorite foods from childhood. At twelve years old I was already hooked on gastronomy and it was an interest that my mother actively encouraged.

The dish made a huge impression on me: crispy potatoes topped with crème fraîche and caviar. We always dipped ours in applesauce, but this—this was latkes through a new lens.

Makes 50 pieces

LATKES

5 pounds russet potatoes, peeled and grated

2 medium Vidalia onions, minced

4 large eggs

4 ounces panko breadcrumbs

0.75 ounce salt

0.5 ounce baking powder

Vegetable oil, for frying

1 (8-ounce) tub crème fraîche

8 ounces salmon roe

1 ounce picked dill

LATKES In a large bowl, mix together the potatoes and onions. Place the mixture in a clean tea towel and wring out as much moisture as you can.

In another large bowl, whisk together the eggs, breadcrumbs, salt and baking powder. Add the potato-onion mixture and mix with your hands until well incorporated.

Heat ¼ inch of vegetable oil in a large skillet over medium-high heat. Scoop 1-tablespoon dollops of the batter into the pan. Squish them down into patty shapes and fry until golden brown, 3 to 4 minutes per side. Repeat with the remaining batter and set the finished latkes aside.

ASSEMBLY Preheat the oven to 350°F.

Place the latkes on large baking sheets and warm them in the oven for 4 minutes. Garnish with dollops of crème fraîche and salmon roe. Sprinkle with the dill. Serve immediately.

CLAMBAKE SHOOTERS

All the flavors of a late summer clambake distilled into a single, savory shot. This shooter is made up of all the elements that would go into a proper clambake—sweet corn, potato, parsley and bacon—cooked and combined with the clam juice, white wine and thyme.

Makes 40 shooters

40 fresh littleneck clams

BROTH
1 tablespoon extra-virgin olive oil
2 garlic cloves, crushed
½ cup chopped yellow onion
7½ cups clam juice
1¼ cups white wine
1 bay leaf
1 lemon, halved
Salt

1½ cups corn kernels, roasted
Extra-virgin olive oil, as needed
8 ounces thick-cut bacon, fried, crumbled
Leaves from 1 bunch flat-leaf parsley

In a tall stockpot with a steamer insert, bring 1 inch of water to a rolling boil. Fill the steamer basket with the clams, lower it into the pot and cover tightly. The clams should open in 4 to 5 minutes.

When all the clams are open, quickly turn them out into a large pan or bowl to cool. Reserve the cooking liquid to use for the broth, adding enough store-bought juice to equal 7½ cups.

BROTH In a tall-sided pot, heat the olive oil over medium heat. Add the garlic and onion. Cook for 2 minutes. Add the clam juice, white wine, bay leaf and lemon halves. Bring to a boil, reduce to a simmer and cook until it has reduced by a quarter in volume. Strain and season with salt to taste. Cool and refrigerate.

ASSEMBLY Lay out all of your shot glasses and place one clam in the bottom of each.

Using a pitcher, fill all the shot glasses with broth, being sure to leave a little room at the top for garnish.

Finish the shots with a few corn kernels, a dash of extra-virgin olive oil, some crumbled bacon and a parsley leaf.

Serve immediately.

_____

CHEF'S NOTES

Put your oven on the lowest possible setting, place all the shot glasses on a sheet pan and put it in the oven for a few minutes before plating this dish. All the glasses will be warm to the touch, and your shooters won't get cold as fast.

Clam cooking liquid can be used as the clam juice, though you may need additional store-bought clam juice to get the proper amount.

CREATING A TEAM

People are everything. My team of chefs, managers planners, cooks, servers, bartenders and dishwashers are the driving force behind OnTheMarc and are a constant source of inspiration and determination for me. I try to cultivate a culture of passion and enthusiasm, with a side of good humor.

Truth be told, I barely look at resumes when I'm hiring someone for my team full time. Instead, I talk to them. I work with them a few times. The information I get from these experiences is far more valuable than reading a curated piece of paper about someone's achievements. I hire based on my gut, asking myself one question every time: will this person go the distance for the good of the team and company? If the answer is yes, I waste no time in getting them on board.

The backgrounds and experience levels that each of my team members have is wide ranging. Some have worked for world-renowned chefs. Some have owned their own businesses and restaurants. Some are industry veterans who know all the tricks of the trade. Others are new to the events industry and bring an incredibly fresh perspective. The richness of knowledge and passion each of them brings to the table never ceases to amaze me.

I take my role very seriously: to guide the team and provide an environment where each can reach their full potential. I genuinely want each employee to love what they do. The more we achieve this as a company, the more we come together as a team, like peas in a pod.

BRAISED SHORT RIB ON CRISPY POTATOES

Makes 40 to 50 pieces

BRAISED SHORT RIBS

2 pounds short ribs, trimmed of any visible fat and cut into 2½-inch cubes

Kosher salt and freshly ground black pepper

2 tablespoons vegetable oil

1 quart chicken stock

4 garlic cloves, smashed

8 ounces chopped yellow onion

8 ounces chopped celery

8 ounces chopped carrot

1 tablespoon tomato paste

1 ounce all-purpose flour

1 cup red wine

SMASHED FINGERLING POTATOES

15 to 20 (3-inch-long) fingerling potatoes

3 tablespoons vegetable oil

Kosher salt

PICKLED HORSERADISH

3 ounces fresh horseradish root, grated on a microplane

7 tablespoons white distilled vinegar

0.1 ounce kosher salt

3 quarts vegetable oil, for frying

1 ounce minced fresh chives

BRAISED SHORT RIBS Preheat the oven to 275°F.

Season the cubed short ribs generously with salt and pepper.

Heat a Dutch oven or other heavy-bottomed pot over medium-high heat and add the vegetable oil. Place a few cubes of short ribs in the pot and sear on all sides. You may need to do this in 3 or 4 batches.

Remove the short ribs to a paper towel-lined plate. Deglaze the pot with a spoonful of the chicken stock and then pour this liquid into a small bowl; set aside.

In the same Dutch oven, combine the garlic, onion, celery and carrots; cook over medium heat for 15 to 20 minutes until they are deeply caramelized. Add the tomato paste and cook for another 3 to 4 minutes or until it is dark reddish-brown in color. Stir in the flour, then add the remaining chicken stock, red wine, short ribs and reserved deglazing liquid.

Cover tightly and transfer the pot to the oven. Braise for 2½ to 3 hours, checking at 2 hours to see if the meat is done. The meat should pull apart easily with a fork, but not fall apart at the touch.

Discard the vegetables. Place the entire Dutch oven in the refrigerator and let it chill overnight.

Take the Dutch oven out of the refrigerator. Remove and discard the hard layer of fat from the top of the pot.

Shred the short ribs, making sure to leave big chunks. Return the shredded meat to the jus in the pot. Cover and refrigerate.

CONTINUED >

SMASHED FINGERLING POTATOES Preheat the oven to 350°F.

Place the fingerling potatoes on a large, rimmed baking sheet and toss with the vegetable oil and salt to taste. Roast for 15 to 20 minutes or until fork tender.

Remove the potatoes from the oven and let them cool slightly, then cut them into 1-inch pieces. Using the flat side of your knife, smash down the potato pieces to an even ⅛-inch thickness. Transfer to an airtight container and refrigerate until needed.

PICKLED HORSERADISH Combine the horse-radish, vinegar and salt in an airtight container. Refrigerate until needed.

ASSEMBLY Heat the oil in a deep fryer to 350°F.

Reheat the short ribs in a small pot with enough jus to cover them.

Drop a few smashed potatoes into the fryer and fry for 1 minute or until golden brown on the edges. Immediately remove them to a paper towel-lined plate to drain. Repeat with the remaining potatoes.

On each fried potato, place a hunk of short rib, a dab of horseradish and sprinkle of chives.

Serve immediately.

CHEF'S NOTES

PRO TIP: Leaving the short ribs in the fridge overnight allows the flavors to marry.

SPECIAL TOOLS: Deep Fryer, Dutch Oven, Microplane

FISH AND CHIPS

Makes 40 to 50 pieces

COD

5 or 6 garlic cloves, smashed

½ bunch dill

8 to 10 slices lemon (approximately 2 lemons)

3 pounds skinless cod fillets, each cut into
3 or 4 equal-size pieces

2 quarts extra-virgin olive oil, or as needed

½ cup capers, chopped

¼ cup minced red onion

¼ cup minced chervil

¼ cup minced fresh chives

2 cups Homemade Mayonnaise (page 214)

Zest and juice of 2 lemons

Salt

40 to 50 Potato Chips (page 216)

¼ cup minced fresh chives

COD Place the garlic, dill and lemon slices in an even layer on the bottom of a Dutch oven. Lay the cod on top of the aromatics and then cover by ½ inch with extra-virgin olive oil.

Place the Dutch oven over low heat, cover and poach the cod until it flakes apart easily, about 10 minutes once it starts bubbling.

Remove the cod to a wire rack and let it cool completely.

When the fish has cooled, place it in a large bowl with the capers, onion, chervil, chives, mayo and lemon zest and juice. Toss gently to combine, trying to leave some big chunks of fish. Season with salt to taste.

Transfer the salad to an airtight container and refrigerate until needed.

ASSEMBLY Scoop about a tablespoon of the cod salad onto a potato chip and garnish with chives.

Serve immediately.

_____

CHEF'S NOTES

You can save the oil to use again a couple more times. Just make sure to cool it with the lid off and then refrigerate it.

Remember to use your mandoline for the potatoes.

These chips will stay crispy for days. As long as they are well sealed, they will even stay crispy in the fridge.

SPECIAL TOOLS: Dutch Oven, Mandoline

STEAK FRITES

Makes 50 pieces

FILET MIGNON

1½ pounds filet mignon, 1 inch thick

Salt and freshly ground black pepper

1 tablespoon extra-virgin olive oil

TATER TOTS

7 large russet potatoes, grated on the large side of a box grater

Salt

3 tablespoons plus 1 teaspoon freshly squeezed lemon juice

3 large eggs, beaten

6½ tablespoons cornstarch

2 ounces minced yellow onion

3 quarts vegetable oil, for frying

Salt and freshly ground black pepper

Whipped Goat Cheese (page 11)

Micro herbs for garnish

FILET MIGNON Preheat the oven to 350°F.

Season the beef on both sides with salt and pepper. Heat a large cast-iron pan over high heat. When the pan just begins to smoke, add the oil and sear the steak for 2 to 3 minutes per side or until a nice crust forms.

Remove the pan from the heat and place the beef on a cutting board. Let the beef rest for half of the total cooking time, then slice it into ¼-inch-thick pieces.

TATER TOTS Preheat the oven to 350°F.

Place the potatoes in a large bowl, season them generously with salt and lemon juice, and let them sit for 20 minutes. Scoop them into a clean tea towel or piece of cheesecloth and wring out as much moisture as you can.

Place the potatoes in a clean bowl and mix them with the eggs, cornstarch and onion. Spread this mixture into a 9 x 13-inch greased baking dish and cover with foil. Bake for 20 minutes. Remove from the oven and set aside to cool.

Cut the potatoes into 1½-inch squares. Set aside.

ASSEMBLY Heat the oil in your deep fryer to 350°F.

Fry a few tater tots for 2 to 3 minutes or until golden brown. Immediately remove them to a paper towel-lined plate and season with salt and pepper. Repeat with the remaining potato squares.

On each tater tot, place a slice of beef, a dollop of whipped goat cheese and some micro herbs for garnish. Serve immediately.

CHEF'S NOTES

SPECIAL TOOLS: Deep Fryer, Cheesecloth

CHAPTER SEVEN

GLUTEN-FULL

There are few things more pleasing to me than good, crusty breads. Any bread with a crunchy exterior and soft, chewy center is the stuff of dreams. Not only great on its own, a quality bread can also be the base for some of the best small bites. In a world full of gluten-free recipes and needs, the bread maven inside of me needed to take a minute to highlight some gluten-full ways to entertain and indulge.

CRAB TOASTS

Makes 40 to 50 pieces

GOCHUJANG CRAB SALAD

1 cup plus 1 tablespoon Homemade Mayonnaise (page 214)

0.5 ounce gochujang

0.5 ounce freshly squeezed lime juice

0.25 ounce fish sauce

3 pounds cooked Dungeness crabmeat, picked over for shells

4 granny smith apples, peeled, cored and small diced

Salt

TOASTS

½ loaf sourdough boule, thinly sliced on an extreme bias

Extra-virgin olive oil

Salt and freshly ground black pepper

1 cup shaved radishes

1 cup sesame seeds, toasted

4 scallions, thinly sliced

1 Granny Smith apple, diced small

GOCHUJANG CRAB SALAD In an airtight container, mix together the mayo, gochujang, lime juice and fish sauce. Fold in the crabmeat and apple; season to taste with salt. Refrigerate until needed.

TOASTS Preheat a grill to high.

Brush the bread slices with olive oil and sprinkle with salt and pepper. Grill for 1 minute per side or until toasted.

ASSEMBLY Heap some crab salad on each piece of toast. Cut the toasts into bite-size pieces and place a few pieces of shaved radish, a sprinkle of sesame seeds, some scallions and a few pieces of apple on each one. Serve immediately.

ORIGINAL GANGSTERS

Getting involved with a company in its infancy is risky. I know that to be true as a client, as an investor and as an employer. Each project brings with it a sharp edge of uncertainty: every new job is the opportunity to succeed or fail. There are two people who took a chance on me at the beginning and for that I am eternally grateful. Amos and Lauren, if I were to ever use the term "original gangster," this would be the time and you would be my "OGs."

When I started catering, it was on my own. I took the phone calls, made the arrangements, prepared the food, talked with the clients and hired the servers, and then, when showtime arrived, tied on my apron and made it happen. I hired other cooks to help me execute the big events. But once the food was eaten and the car was packed, it was just me again. I didn't mind it. In fact, I liked the Zen of doing the dishes alone.

Hiring and retaining staff will forever be the single greatest challenge of owning my own business. In 2009, I met Amos. One of the ads I'd placed on Craigslist was for hourly cooks and he responded. I didn't even interview him before we worked our first big party together. He stood out from the other cooks. I could tell that he had talent. I hired him the next week.

And then there were two! I now had a counterpart with whom I would work, grapple, create and grow.

Shortly after Amos began working with me full time, more time opened up for me to focus on the thing that truly distinguishes OnTheMarc: the event planning process. That's when Lauren joined the team.

Lauren was already a part-time server for the company. She always stuck out in my mind—a natural leader who always showed a tremendous amount of initiative regardless of the circumstances. Her commitment, polish, attention to detail and relaxed professionalism with our clients gave me zero reason not to hire her full time. In fact, I would've been foolish not to. Soon she joined Amos and I as the third member of our very lean team. It was so nice to finally have a team of people rather than being a one-man band.

My first and second full-time hires are still by my side, leading OnTheMarc into the future. Neither has ever hit a ceiling of capability or been unable to handle any task I throw at them. They have grown with their roles to meet the demands of the expanding business. Since 2009, Amos is the only person apart from me that has held the title of "Executive Chef" at OnTheMarc and Lauren has risen to be my Director of Sales.

When I hired Amos and Lauren, the risks were mutual. I was making a financial commitment to them that I couldn't back out of and they, in return, trusted me to grow the business to be a secure, successful place to work. The opportunity to work with each of them, while extremely stressful and daunting at first, has been incredibly gratifying. I feel nothing but appreciation for all they have brought to the business and the journey we have traveled together.

Amos and Lauren, my OGs, here's to continuing the great journey. Thank you!

TOMATO AND MOZZARELLA PANINI

Makes 50 pieces

PESTO

1 bunch basil, leaves and tender stems

5 tablespoons freshly squeezed lemon juice

⅓ cup grated Parmesan cheese

⅓ cup pine nuts

2 garlic cloves, smashed

1½ teaspoons Dijon mustard

¼ cup ice cubes

1 cup extra-virgin olive oil

2 ficelles, sliced into 100 (⅛-inch-thick) pieces

1 pound Roma tomatoes, cut into ⅛-inch-thick slices, then into 1 x 1-inch squares

1 (1-pound) ball fresh mozzarella, cut into ⅛-inch-thick slices, then into 1 x 1-inch squares

½ cup extra-virgin olive oil, for brushing

½ cup balsamic reduction, for drizzling

PESTO Combine all the ingredients in a blender except the oil.

Blend on high speed until smooth, then, with the motor running, slowly drizzle in the oil. You may have to use the plunger to help the pesto move in the blender.

ASSEMBLY Preheat the oven to 350°F.

Lay 50 of the ficelle slices on a large baking sheet. Put one piece of tomato, one piece of cheese and a squeeze of pesto on top of each. Top with another slice of ficelle and set aside. Repeat for the remaining panini.

Brush the panini on both sides with extra-virgin olive oil and heat them in the oven for 4 minutes or until the cheese melts.

Drizzle with the balsamic reduction and serve immediately.

———————————

CHEF'S NOTES

Place the pesto in a squeeze bottle for making dollops easily. Freeze all your extra pesto. You can use it in pastas or as a salad dressing or dip.

CONFIT CHICKEN AND APPLE PANINI

If you're Jewish, you definitely know about the power of schmaltz (chicken fat).

We confit our chicken in schmaltz for this mini panini to pack in as much flavor as possible and heighten the richness of each bite. Schmaltz is probably one of the most underrated cooking fats, but I can tell you confidently it deserves a podium. And you'll love the panini, too.

Makes 50 panini

CONFIT CHICKEN SALAD

4 chicken thighs

2 tablespoons vegetable oil

6 cups chicken fat

½ cup grated aged Cheddar cheese

5 medium Granny Smith apples, peeled and grated

2 ficelles, each cut into 100 (⅛-inch-thick) slices

1 (17.6-ounce) wheel Brie cheese, cut into 1-inch-long, ⅛-inch-thick pieces

Extra-virgin olive oil

½ cup Tomato Molasses Reduction (page 92)

CONFIT CHICKEN THIGHS Preheat the oven to 250°F. Brown the thighs in a sauté pan over high heat with the vegetable oil for 2 to 3 minutes per side. Cover the browned chicken thighs in chicken fat (schmaltz) in a baking dish or Dutch over and bake for 90 minutes.

CHICKEN SALAD Cool the confit chicken and pick all the meat off the bones.

Place the chicken in a food processor along with the Cheddar and apple; pulse until just combined.

ASSEMBLY Preheat the oven to 350°F.

Using a 100 scoop, which is 0.33 ounce, top half of the bread slices with the chicken mixture and one slice of Brie, then top with another piece of bread. Brush both sides of the panini with extra-virgin olive oil, place them on large, rimmed baking sheets and heat in the oven for 3 to 4 minutes or until the cheese melts. Drizzle with the tomato molasses reduction and serve immediately.

CHEF'S NOTES

SPECIAL TOOLS: 100 Scoop

SMOKED SALMON CROQUE MONSIEUR

When I was at the CIA, Amanda Hesser published a piece in the *New York Times* about Le Bernardin's croque monsieur. The sandwich she described is just a grilled cheese, but one that happens to contain sliced smoked salmon and a considerable portion of sturgeon caviar. Here's how we play with this idea at OnTheMarc.

Makes 40 pieces

1½ cups unsalted butter, for brushing and cooking

20 slices white Pullman bread

2 cups Béchamel (page 212)

10 slices Jarlsberg Swiss cheese

1 pound smoked salmon

8 ounces salmon roe

1 tablespoon minced fresh chives

Melt the butter in a small saucepan over low heat; set aside.

Lay all the bread slices on a clean surface and put 1 tablespoon of béchamel on each slice, spreading it evenly with a spatula.

Put one piece of cheese and enough smoked salmon to cover 10 bread slices, then cover with another slice of bread. You should have 10 completed sandwiches.

Brush both sides of each sandwich with the melted butter and lay them on parchment-lined baking sheets.

Cover and refrigerate.

ASSEMBLY On a griddle or cast-iron pan over medium heat, sear the grilled cheese sandwiches for 3 to 4 minutes per side, or until they are golden brown and the cheese is melted.

Once the sandwiches are done, let them rest on your cutting board for 2 minutes so that cheese does not spill out when you cut them.

Using a sharp bread knife, cut the crust off two sides of each sandwich and then cut each sandwich into 4 finger-sized pieces. Top with the roe and chives.

Serve immediately.

_____

CHEF'S NOTES

A hot pot can still scorch your béchamel after it's removed from the stove, so once the béchamel is seasoned, transfer it into another container as soon as possible.

MICRO GRILLED CHEESE WITH TOMATO SOUP DIPPING SAUCE

Everybody loves this hors d'oeuvre, probably because it is comfort food at its finest. We are sneaky with our use of béchamel in this one, but it's the difference between a good grilled cheese and a great one. The béchamel adds an unctuousness that sliced cheese can't provide and acts as our insurance policy for both decadence and griddled perfection.

Makes 40 pieces

TOMATO SOUP

3 ounces unsalted butter

2 medium yellow onions

2 garlic cloves, chopped

24 ounces whole peeled canned tomatoes

3 cups vegetable stock

2 teaspoons kosher salt

¼ teaspoon freshly ground black pepper

SANDWICHES

1½ cups unsalted butter, for brushing and cooking

20 slices white bread (Pullman loaf or pain de mie)

2 cups Béchamel (page 212)

10 slices (1½ pounds) Jarlsberg Swiss cheese

TOMATO SOUP Melt the butter in a saucepan over medium heat, then add the onions and garlic. Cook, stirring frequently, for 15 minutes until the vegetables are very soft. Add the tomatoes, vegetable stock, salt and pepper and bring the mixture to a boil. Reduce to a simmer and cook for about 20 minutes.

Transfer the soup to a blender and blend on high speed until smooth.

Cool and refrigerate in an airtight container.

SANDWICHES Melt the butter in a small saucepan over low heat; set aside.

Lay all the bread slices on a clean surface and put 1 tablespoon of béchamel on each slice, spreading it evenly with a spatula.

Put one piece of cheese on 10 slices of the bread and cover with another slice of bread. You should have 10 completed sandwiches.

Brush both sides of each sandwich with the melted butter and lay them on parchment-lined baking sheets.

Cover and refrigerate.

CONTINUED >

ASSEMBLY In a medium saucepan over medium heat, warm the tomato soup to a gentle simmer.

On a griddle or cast-iron pan over medium heat, sear the grilled cheese sandwiches for 3 to 4 minutes per side, or until they are a golden brown and the cheese is melted.

Once the sandwiches are done, let them rest on your cutting board for 2 minutes so that cheese does not spill out when you cut them.

Using a sharp serrated bread knife, cut the crust off two sides of each sandwich and then cut each sandwich into 4 finger-sized pieces.

Serve immediately.

CHEF'S NOTES

A hot pot can still scorch your béchamel after it's removed from the stove, so once the béchamel is seasoned, transfer it into another container as soon as possible.

Use a 1-inch circle cutter to get the small rounded shape.

CUBAN CROQUE MADAME

Makes 40 pieces

SANDWICHES

1½ cups unsalted butter, for brushing and cooking

2 cups Béchamel (page 212)

4 tablespoons Dijon mustard

20 slices country white Pullman bread

20 slices (1½ pounds) Jarlsberg Swiss cheese

40 slices (2 pounds) smoked ham

60 pieces Pickled Cucumber (page 219)

MOJO SAUCE

2 cups fresh lime juice

2 cups fresh orange juice

2 teaspoons dried oregano

2 teaspoons cumin

1 head garlic, peeled and crushed

½ cup ice

1⅓ cup olive oil

40 quail eggs

SANDWICHES Melt the butter in a small saucepan over low heat and reserve.

Stir the Dijon mustard into the béchamel and set aside. Lay out all the bread on a clean surface and put 1 tablespoon of the béchamel-mustard mixture on each slice, spreading it evenly with a spatula. Put 1 piece of Swiss cheese, 2 slices of ham and 6 slices of pickle on 10 slices of the bread; finish with the matching slice of bread. You should have 10 completed sandwiches.

Brush both sides of each sandwich with melted butter and lay them on a parchment-lined baking sheet. Cover and refrigerate.

MOJO SAUCE Combine all the ingredients except the ice and oil in a blender and blend on high speed until smooth, then strain it through a fine-mesh sieve into a small saucepan. Bring it to a boil, then reduce the heat to low and simmer for 15 minutes, uncovered, until it has reduced to a thick consistency. Transfer to a blender, add the ice and blend on high speed while streaming in the oil. Cover and refrigerate until needed.

ASSEMBLY On a griddle or cast-iron pan over medium heat, sear the grilled cheese sandwiches for 3 to 4 minutes per side, or until they are golden brown and the cheese is melted.

Once the sandwiches are done, let them rest on your cutting board for 2 minutes so that cheese does not spill out when you cut them.

Using a sharp bread knife, cut the crust off two sides of each sandwich and then cut each sandwich into 4 finger-sized pieces.

On the same griddle, fry the quail eggs in butter until sunny-side up, about 45 seconds.

Lay one quail egg on each sandwich piece and drizzle with the mojo sauce. Serve immediately.

FRONT YARD FARMER

It all started with an obsession over Italian zucchini. I couldn't find the kind I had tried in Italy in the States, so I decided I'd try to grow them. Now, I grow as many herbs and vegetables as I can each year. It's an essential skill set for chefs: understanding how our food grows by going through the seasons with actual crops.

The amount of knowledge I've gained from keeping my own chef's garden has given me a firsthand, deep appreciation for farmers. Not only is the work physically demanding, but each crop variety also comes with a unique set of challenges and requirements. Why you plant certain vegetables in a certain spot, how this year has differed in experience with similar varieties from last year—it is all very strategic. Not too different from my business or a game of chess, in a sense.

Like running a company, each day in the garden brings a new challenge or offers new lessons. You're constantly chasing highs and lows. I am reminded that there is only so much you can control, like mischief made by a ravenous racoon, and that, despite my willingness to be a part of it all, trusting the process is good, too. I've come to expect a dynamic experience with my garden—the need to adapt, the problem solving and the fun of strategizing each year and throughout each season. At the very least, the constant availability of fresh herbs is, hands down, my favorite (garden) work perk.

FOUR SEASONS BRUSCHETTA

The concept of topping crusty, grilled bread with simple ingredients was not foreign to me as a kid. One of my favorite childhood snacks was the very simple bruschetta my mom made easily and often: fresh basil, canned tomato, salt, olive oil.

When I worked at the Sheraton in high school, this idea of bruschetta as an elevated food came to the forefront of my curious mind. One day, I saw one of the lead cooks make some. Like my mom's, this had tomato and basil, but he added fresh mozzarella and used fresh Roma tomatoes. It looked fantastic—colorful and lively—and I think you'd be hard-pressed to find someone who would object to the addition of fresh mozzarella to most anything.

As a curious culinary kid with constantly racing thoughts, I often found myself surprised by the simplest of concepts. "Why didn't I think of that sooner?" played over and over in my internal monologue. I began to think more broadly about what could be called bruschetta, and that's still what we do at OTM today. We are consistently inspired by the seasons, and a crunchy, chewy piece of bread is a great way to showcase that. For the home cook, bruschetta is a great way to use up leftovers and clean out the fridge. It can be elegant, it can be functional, it can be fun.

PEA, MINT AND BACON BRUSCHETTA

Makes 48 pieces

PEA PURÉE

3 cups cooked fresh peas, divided

2 teaspoons salt

Zest and juice of 2 lemons

1 tablespoon finely chopped mint

¼ cup extra-virgin olive oil

6 slices bacon, cut into lardons, fried until crispy and fat has rendered out

12 slices whole-wheat bread, each cut into 4 triangles

Extra-virgin olive oil

Salt and freshly ground black pepper

0.5 ounce minced fresh chives

1 bunch pea tendrils, for garnish

PEA PURÉE Place half the peas in a large bowl and set aside.

Put the remaining peas in a food processor along with the salt, lemon zest and juice, mint and extra-virgin olive oil. Purée until smooth. Transfer the purée to the bowl with the whole peas, add the bacon, and mix well. Set aside.

ASSEMBLY Preheat the oven to 350°F. Drizzle the bread triangles with oil, season with salt and pepper and place them on large, rimmed baking sheets. Toast in the oven until crisp, about 5 minutes.

Remove the toasts from the oven, place a spoonful of the pea mixture on each toast point and sprinkle with the chives and pea tendrils. Serve immediately.

HEIRLOOM TOMATO AND CHICKPEA BRUSCHETTA

Makes 40 to 50 pieces

TOMATO-CHICKPEA TOPPING

1 (15-ounce) can chickpeas, drained, divided

1½ pounds heirloom tomatoes, cut into medium-size dice

2 tablespoons minced garlic

½ cup chopped fresh basil

1 tablespoon freshly squeezed lemon juice

1½ tablespoons extra-virgin olive oil, divided

2 teaspoons salt

¼ teaspoon crushed red pepper flakes

40 to 50 (¾-inch-square) slices ciabatta

Extra-virgin olive oil

Salt and freshly ground black pepper

0.5 ounce minced fresh chives

TOMATO-CHICKPEA TOPPING Preheat the oven to 350°F.

Coarsely chop half of the chickpeas and mix them with the tomatoes, garlic, basil, lemon juice, ½ tablespoon of the olive oil and salt; toss well and set aside.

Toss the second half of the chickpeas with the crushed red pepper and remaining 1 tablespoon extra-virgin olive oil; sprinkle with salt. Spread this mixture on a rimmed baking sheet and roast for 15 to 20 minutes or until crunchy. Remove from the oven and let the chickpeas cool; crush coarsely using the bottom of a pot.

ASSEMBLY Preheat a grill to high. Drizzle each piece of ciabatta with extra-virgin olive oil, season with salt and pepper and grill until crisp, about 2 minutes per side.

Place a spoonful of tomato-chickpea topping on each piece of ciabatta, sprinkle with the crispy chickpeas and top with some chives. Serve immediately.

WILD MUSHROOM AND HERB BRUSCHETTA

Makes 40 to 50 pieces

MUSHROOM AND HERB TOPPING

5 tablespoons extra-virgin olive oil, divided

1 pound oyster mushrooms

1 pound shiitake mushrooms

1 pound shallots, chopped

4 ounces baby arugula

2 tablespoons champagne vinegar

1 tablespoon truffle oil

1 teaspoon chopped fresh flat-leaf parsley

1 teaspoon chopped fresh chervil

40 to 50 (¾-inch-square) slices sourdough bread

Extra-virgin olive oil

Salt and freshly ground black pepper

0.5 ounce minced fresh chives

MUSHROOM AND HERB TOPPING Heat 2 tablespoons of the extra-virgin olive oil in a large skillet over medium heat and sauté the mushrooms for about 9 minutes or until browned and soft. Cool and reserve.

Heat 2 more tablespoons of oil in another large skillet over medium heat and sauté the shallots for about 10 minutes or until golden and soft. Cool and reserve.

In a large bowl, toss together the arugula, champagne vinegar, truffle oil, parsley, chervil, the remaining 1 tablespoon of oil and the cooked mushrooms and shallots.

ASSEMBLY Preheat the oven to 350°F.

Drizzle each sourdough crostini with olive oil and season with salt and pepper. Place the crostini on large baking sheets and toast in the oven for 4 to 5 minutes.

Remove from the oven and put a spoonful of the mushroom topping on each crostini. Sprinkle with chives. Serve immediately.

BEET, BLUEBERRIES AND GOAT CHEESE BRUSCHETTA

Makes 48 pieces

BEET TOPPING

1 pound blanched beets, peeled and finely diced (see note)

1 cup Pickled Blueberries (see page 220)

4 ounces goat cheese, crumbled

2 tablespoons white balsamic vinegar

3 tablespoons extra-virgin olive oil

2 teaspoons minced shallot

2 teaspoons salt

12 slices pumpernickel bread

Extra-virgin olive oil

Salt and freshly ground black pepper

0.5 ounce minced fresh chives

BEET TOPPING In a large bowl, combine the beets, blueberries, goat cheese, balsamic vinegar, olive oil, shallot and salt. Toss gently to prevent the cheese from breaking up too much.

ASSEMBLY Preheat the oven to 350°F.

Cut each pumpernickel slice into 4 triangles. Drizzle each piece with olive oil, season with salt and pepper and place them on large, rimmed baking sheets. Toast in the oven for 4 to 5 minutes or until crisp.

Remove from the oven and place a spoonful of the topping on each piece of toast. Sprinkle with chives and serve immediately.

CHEF'S NOTES

Candy Striped Beets are used here, but any variety of beet will do!

To cook whole beets, first give them a good scrubbing, then place them in a large pot with enough cold water to cover. Bring to a boil, then reduce the heat and simmer for 40 minutes, covered, until the beets are easily pierced with the tip of a knife. Remove from the water and rub off the skins with a paper towel.

CHAPTER EIGHT

OLD & NEW

I'm lucky to come from a long line of self-made family members, all of whom have sage advice about business and life. Whenever I find myself in need of some wisdom, I call my grandfather. He has counseled me through my toughest times as a young business owner.

Comparing experiences across generations is essential to keeping a balanced perspective—a lesson I've already begun to share with my son Ethan. Some things change, ideas become updated or defunct, and some things are steadfast.

The way people once ate and how my clients want to eat today are in many ways different. The thing I've noticed the most, though, is the want for new, lighter versions of old, heavier favorites.

One of the ways I accommodate this is with "choux buns." These light and airy, steam-risen buns are great for hors d'oeuvres and for clients with an affinity for the old and new.

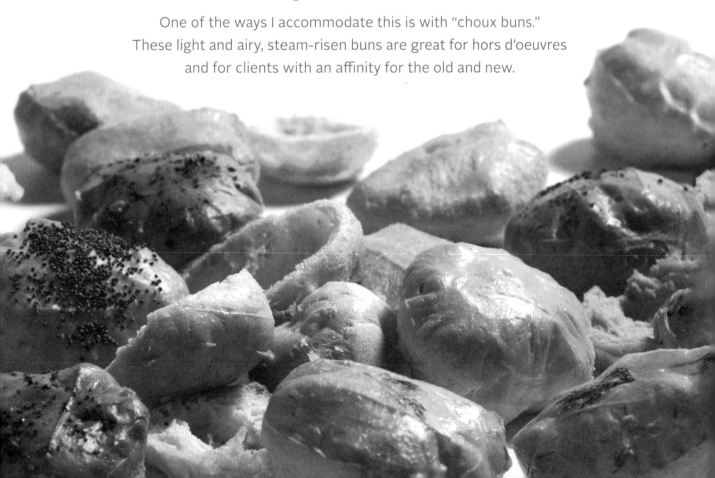

MINI BLTS

Few sandwiches are more loved than the classic bacon, lettuce and tomato. Even when our BLTs are miniaturized, I always want to make sure they pack as much flavor as a full-sized version. To that end, we include bacon fat in the pâte à choux bun to give it smoky richness, we oven-dry the tomatoes to concentrate their flavor and we cook thick-cut bacon in the oven to ensure that it is perfectly crisped.

Makes 40 to 50 sandwiches

1 recipe Basic Pâte à Choux (page 218), made with bacon fat

OVEN-DRIED KUMATOES

20 ounces kumato tomatoes, sliced ¼ inch thick

4 garlic cloves, minced

2 sprigs fresh thyme

0.15 ounce salt

4½ teaspoons extra-virgin olive oil

Pinch of freshly ground black pepper

30 strips thick-cut bacon

1 head iceberg lettuce, shredded

1½ cups Homemade Mayonnaise (page 214)

PÂTE À CHOUX Follow the directions for Basic Pâte à Choux on page 217, using the same amount of bacon fat (4 ounces) in place of the butter. Let the baked buns cool to room temperature.

OVEN-DRIED KUMATOES Reduce the oven temperature to 275°F. Line a large rimmed baking sheet with parchment paper.

Place the tomatoes in a large bowl with the rest of the ingredients. Toss well, then spread the mixture on the prepared baking sheet in a single layer. Transfer the baking sheet to the oven and let the tomatoes dehydrate on the non-convection bake setting for 45 to 50 minutes. (If your oven does not have this setting, the tomatoes will cook faster by about 10 minutes.)

Remove the baking sheet from the oven, let the tomatoes cool and transfer them to an airtight container. Refrigerate until ready to use.

CONTINUED >

Preheat the oven to 350°F. Line a rimmed baking sheet with parchment paper.

Spread the bacon slices on the prepared baking sheet in a single layer. Transfer to the oven and bake for 6 to 8 minutes or until crisp. Remove the bacon to a paper towel-lined plate to drain, then cut each strip into 4 equal pieces. Set aside. Keep the oven on.

ASSEMBLY Split open a bun and put a few strips of bacon and one slice of tomato inside. (You can open and fill all the buns like this a couple of hours before the party and leave them in the fridge.)

Place the filled sandwiches on rimmed baking sheets and bake for 3 minutes or until warmed through. Remove the sandwiches from the oven and add some lettuce and a dollop of mayo in each one.

Serve hot.

KOBE SLIDERS

Makes 40 to 50 pieces

MINI KOBE BURGERS

5 pounds ground Kobe beef

CARAMELIZED ONIONS

2 to 3 tablespoons vegetable oil

2 medium yellow onions, cut into small dice

Kosher salt

1 recipe Basic Pâte à Choux (page 218)

1½ cups OnTheMarc Signature Ketchup (page 214)

1 pound Manchego cheese, sliced

Salt and freshly ground pepper

Vegetable oil, for cooking the burgers

MINI KOBE BURGERS Form the ground beef into 40 to 50 balls (about 1.5 ounces each), being careful not to overwork the meat.

Lay the balls on a parchment-lined baking sheet. Cover and refrigerate for later.

CARAMELIZED ONIONS Place the oil in a medium sauté pan over low heat.

Once the pan is hot, add the diced onions with a pinch of salt and cook over low heat for 20 to 25 minutes, stirring frequently, until the onions are a deep brown color and taste rich and sweet.

Remove the pan from the heat, let the onions cool, and store them in an airtight container in the refrigerator until ready to use.

ASSEMBLY Preheat the oven to 350°F. Place a medium sauté pan over medium-high heat. Meanwhile, cut open the buns and put some caramelized onions, a squirt of ketchup and a slice of cheese inside each one.

Generously season a few of the mini Kobe patties with salt and pepper, add some vegetable oil to the sauté pan and drop the patties into the hot oil. Cook for about 2 minutes per side for medium (135°F internal temperature), or longer for medium-well (140°F internal temperature). Immediately remove the burgers from the pan and place them into the prepared buns. Repeat with the remaining patties.

When all the burgers are cooked and in the buns, place the filled buns on rimmed baking sheets and bake for 3 to 4 minutes or until warmed through. Remove from the oven and serve immediately.

SALMON SLIDERS

On certain occasions, beef sliders or BLTs are right for the crowd. On certain occasions, they're not. Enter our salmon sliders, more delicately flavored yet still substantial. Perfect for brunches, showers and luncheons, the salmon is topped with a savory artichoke aioli and served in a dill choux bun.

Makes 40 to 50 sandwiches

ARTICHOKE AIOLI

1 garlic clove

2 large eggs

0.5 ounce Dijon mustard

0.2 ounce kosher salt

4½ teaspoons freshly squeezed lemon juice

4½ teaspoons white vinegar

¼ cup extra-virgin olive oil

6 ounces marinated artichoke hearts, well drained

1 cup plus 1 tablespoon vegetable oil

4 pounds skinless salmon fillets

Salt

1 (5-ounce) bag mizuna

1 lemon, halved

Extra-virgin olive oil

1 recipe Dill Pâte à Choux (page 218)

ARTICHOKE AIOLI Combine everything except the vegetable oil in the blender and blend on medium speed for 30 to 40 seconds until smooth. Increase the speed to high and drizzle in the vegetable oil in a steady stream until the mixture emulsifies.

Transfer the aioli to an airtight container and store it in the refrigerator until ready to use.

Preheat the oven to 350°F. Line 2 large baking sheets with parchment paper. Check the salmon for any leftover scales and pin bones, and remove them.

Lay the salmon fillets on the prepared baking sheets and brush them generously on both sides with some of the artichoke aioli. Season with salt.

Bake the salmon for 20 minutes or until it flakes easily with a fork. Remove from the oven and flake the salmon after cooking, while it's still hot. Do not turn off the oven.

CONTINUED >

ASSEMBLY Place the mizuna in a large bowl and squeeze some fresh lemon juice on top. Add a drizzle of olive oil and a pinch of salt, then toss to coat. Check the seasoning and add more lemon, oil or salt as needed.

Split open each bun, put about 1.5 ounces of cooked salmon inside and place on a large baking sheet. Transfer the filled buns to the oven and heat for 4 minutes, then immediately remove them from the oven, add a pinch of mizuna to each slider and serve hot.

CHEF'S NOTES

Adding some fresh dill and chives to the mizuna salad will accentuate the herbs in the bun and create layers of flavor.

You can flake all the salmon ahead of time to make things easier.

BBQ BRISKET PO'BOYS

I love brisket. I have loved it since I could eat solid food. Brisket is served at most Jewish High Holidays and I gladly join in the feast each time.

As a chef, not only do I relish the idea of sharing brisket with my clients, but it is also a very practical food. What's great about serving this dish to guests is that, because the meat is already cooked low and slow, you don't have to worry about hitting a specific temperature. Whenever we need one at OTM, we cook an entire brisket; if you're making a small portion at home, you can use the fattier side of the second cut brisket. The only real trick here is to cook the brisket—really cook it—until a knife is met with almost no resistance.

Makes 40 to 50 pieces

BBQ BRISKET

4 pounds beef brisket, cleaned

3 cups BBQ Rub (page 222)

6 tablespoons vegetable oil, divided

3 cups chicken stock

4 garlic cloves, smashed

8 ounces chopped celery

8 ounces chopped yellow onion

8 ounces chopped carrot

1 ounce tomato paste

1 ounce all-purpose flour

1 cup BBQ Sauce (page 212)

CABBAGE AND CARROT SLAW

5⅓ cups thinly sliced or shredded green cabbage

2⅔ cups thinly sliced or shredded red cabbage

½ medium carrot, peeled and grated

2 tablespoons Homemade Mayonnaise (page 214)

Salt

1 recipe Corn Pâte à Choux (page 218)

Pickled Cucumbers (page 219)

BBQ BRISKET Prepare the day before.

Preheat the oven to 275°F.

Dust the brisket all over with the BBQ rub.

Heat 4 tablespoons of the vegetable oil in a large Dutch oven over medium heat. When the oil is hot, sear the brisket on both sides until browned. Transfer the meat to a plate, then deglaze the pot with a few spoonfuls of the chicken stock and pour this hot liquid into a bowl. Set aside.

Wipe out the pot, place it back over medium heat and add the remaining 2 tablespoons vegetable oil. When the oil is hot, add the garlic, celery, onion and carrot and sauté for 10 to 15 minutes or until deeply caramelized.

Now, add the tomato paste and cook for 4 to 5 minutes, until it turns a deep reddish-brown color. Add the flour, stir to incorporate and then deglaze the pot with the remaining chicken stock. Add the BBQ sauce, brisket and reserved deglazing liquid and cover the pot.

CONTINUED >

Transfer the pot to the oven and braise the brisket for 3 to 4 hours or until fork tender. Check it at 2 hours just to make sure it isn't cooking faster than expected.

Remove the brisket from the oven, let it cool to room temperature and refrigerate overnight.

The next day, discard the hard layer of fat on top.

Cut the brisket lengthwise into three or four 2-inch-wide strips, depending on the size of the brisket. Cut these long piece into ⅛-inch-thick slices.

Return the brisket slices to the jus, cover the pot and refrigerate until ready to use.

CABBAGE AND CARROT SLAW In a large bowl, combine the green and red cabbage, carrot and mayonnaise. Toss well to combine and season with salt. Set aside.

ASSEMBLY Preheat the oven to 350°F.

Place the brisket in the oven and let it reheat for 15 minutes. (Or, if you have more time, reheat the brisket on the stovetop over medium-low heat.)

Split open the buns, place them on rimmed baking sheets, and bake for 2 minutes or until heated through.

Put a slice of brisket, a tablespoon of slaw and a pickle inside each bun.

Serve immediately.

MUSHROOM BURGERS

Until my executive chef Amos showed me otherwise, I truly did not believe that a good veggie burger could exist. This recipe came about as many have: a client requested a "Burger Trio Bar" and I racked my brain for the third burger option. Beef and tuna came easy, but I struggled with the concept of making a veggie burger that people would enjoy. Amos deserves all the credit for creating these sliders—primarily mushroom and quinoa—that are downright delicious.

When we serve these at parties, some guests are surprised to find out after the fact that the burger patties weren't, in fact, made of beef. Even people who wouldn't normally choose a veggie burger like them. We love them with pickled onion, aged Cheddar and smashed avocado, but toppings are chef's choice. Once you add salt to the mixture, you have thirty minutes to form the sliders and either deep fry them or freeze them.

Makes 40 to 50 pieces

MUSHROOM BURGERS

2 tablespoons paprika

2 tablespoons onion powder

2 tablespoons garlic powder

8 ounces cornstarch

Kosher salt

2½ pounds cremini (a.k.a. baby bella) mushrooms, thinly sliced

1 medium yellow onion, minced

5 large eggs, beaten

4 cups cooked red quinoa

½ bunch flat-leaf parsley, finely chopped

Sherry vinegar

3 quarts vegetable oil, for frying

SMASHED AVOCADO

3 ripe avocados, halved, pits removed

1 tablespoon plus 1 teaspoon freshly squeezed lemon juice

1 ounce minced yellow onion

2 teaspoons extra-virgin olive oil

Kosher salt

1 recipe Paprika Basic Pâte à Choux (page 218)

2 pounds aged Cheddar cheese, thinly sliced

Pickled Red Onions (page 221)

3 heads Bibb lettuce, cut into quarters depending on size

CONTINUED >

MUSHROOM BURGERS Line 2 half sheet pans with parchment paper. Combine all the dry ingredients in a large bowl; mix thoroughly, add the wet ingredients and mix to combine. Dip a clean 2-ounce ice cream scoop into boiling water and scoop 40 to 50 balls of the mushroom mixture onto the prepared baking sheets. The balls should be close together but not touching. Cover the baking sheets with aluminum foil and freeze the patties for 4 to 5 hours.

Heat the oil in your deep fryer to 350°F. Fry the frozen burgers for 2 to 3 minutes. They will still be a little raw in the center. Remove the burgers from the fryer and set aside on a paper towel-lined plate to drain.

SMASHED AVOCADO Combine the avocados, lemon juice, onion and olive oil in a large bowl and use your hands or a whisk to smash everything together. Season to taste with salt.

ASSEMBLY Preheat the oven to 350°F.

Cut open each bun and put a mushroom burger and a slice of Cheddar inside. Place the burgers on rimmed baking sheets and bake for 5 minutes or until heated through.

Remove from the oven and add some pickled onion, smashed avocado and lettuce to each burger. Serve immediately.

CHEF'S NOTES

SPECIAL TOOLS: Deep Fryer

VEAL PARMESAN MEATBALLS

Makes 50 pieces

1½ pounds ground veal

½ recipe Basic Pâte à Choux (page 218)

1½ cups Tomato Jam (page 215)

1 (8-ounce) ball mozzarella cheese, diced

Vegetable oil

Salt and pepper to taste

½ cup chiffonade of basil

Form the veal into meatballs the size of large grapes. Set aside.

Preheat the oven to 350°F.

Split all buns in half. Add a spoonful of tomato jam and a cube of mozzarella to each bun. Place the buns on rimmed baking sheets.

Place a griddle over medium heat and brush it with vegetable oil.

Season a few meatballs with salt and pepper and sear them until golden on all sides.

While the meatballs cook, warm the buns in the oven for 4 minutes or just until the cheese melts.

Put a hot meatball inside each bun and garnish with basil. Serve immediately.

CHAPTER NINE

MICRO BUTCHERY

Every guest has a notion of what an hors d'oeuvre is. This is what makes selecting a list of small bites for an event so challenging—you always want every person to have at least one or two bites of something they love. In my experience, as often as we get requests for vegan or vegetarian hors d'oeuvres, we field requests for double Kobe cocktail franks and multiple meat options. There's always a contingency of guests who love a bite-sized canapé with meat as the centerpiece.

Just because the bites are small doesn't mean we don't take the same care and attention as we do with dinner portions when preparing filet mignon for "steak frites" or lamb pops as an hors d'oeuvre. Carnivores are delighted by our commitment to quality when they're greeted with the contents of this chapter.

STEAK TOSTADAS

Makes 50 pieces

SALSA FRESCA

2 dried guajillo chiles

1 cup water

2 plum tomatoes, halved

1 red bell pepper, stemmed and seeded

½ jalapeño pepper, stemmed and seeded

2 garlic cloves, peeled

1 small red onion, halved and peeled

½ teaspoon Mexican Seasoning (page 223)

5 ounces freshly squeezed lime juice

14¼ ounces vegetable oil

Salt

CORN SALSA

2 teaspoons vegetable oil

2.75 ounces fresh sweet corn kernels

1.75 ounces finely diced red bell pepper

1.75 ounces finely diced red onion

2.25 ounces crumbled queso fresco cheese

0.2 ounce finely chopped fresh cilantro

BAVETTE STEAK

1 pound bavette beef steak

Salt and freshly ground black pepper

Mexican Seasoning (page 223)

1 tablespoon extra-virgin olive oil

TOSTADAS

3 quarts vegetable oil, for frying

3 (12-inch-diameter) flour tortillas

½ cup chopped fresh cilantro

SALSA FRESCA Preheat the oven to 450°F.

Remove the seeds and toast the guajillos in a hot pan for 10 seconds, then transfer them to a small saucepan, cover with the water and let them rehydrate over high heat for 3 to 4 minutes. Remove the pan from the heat. Set aside.

Combine the tomatoes, bell pepper, jalapeño, garlic and red onion on a large, rimmed baking sheet and spread the mixture out in a single layer. Roast until charred and soft, about 10 minutes.

Remove the vegetables from the oven and let them cool slightly, then add them to a blender along with the guajillo chiles and their soaking liquid, the Mexican seasoning, lime juice and vegetable oil. Blend on high speed until smooth. Taste and add salt and more lime juice as necessary.

CORN SALSA Heat the oil in a large skillet over high heat, add the corn and cook for 2 to 3 minutes, stirring constantly, until the corn is charred. Remove the skillet from the heat and set it aside to cool. When the corn has cooled to room temperature, place it in a large bowl and toss with the bell pepper, onion, cheese and cilantro. Cover and refrigerate until needed.

CONTINUED >

BAVETTE STEAK Preheat the oven to 350°F.

Season the beef on both sides with salt, pepper and Mexican seasoning. Heat a large cast-iron pan over high heat. When the pan just begins to smoke, add the oil and sear the steak for 2 minutes per side or until a nice crust forms.

Remove the pan from the oven and place the beef on a cutting board.

Let the beef rest for half of the total cooking time, then slice it into ⅛-inch-thick pieces.

TOSTADAS Heat the oil in your deep fryer to 350°F. Using a 2-inch round biscuit or cookie cutter, punch 2-inch tortillas out of larger store-bought tortillas. Fry the tortillas for 1–2 minutes or until golden brown. Immediately remove them to a paper towel-lined plate.

ASSEMBLY On each tostada, place a slice of beef, 1 tablespoon of corn salsa, a dollop of salsa fresca and some cilantro. Serve immediately.

CHEF'S NOTES

SPECIAL TOOLS: Deep Fryer, 2-inch Round Biscuit or Cookie Cutter

OSSO BUCCO ON PANISSE

Makes 40 to 50 pieces

BRAISED OSSO BUCCO

4 pounds veal osso bucco

Salt and freshly ground black pepper

2 tablespoons extra-virgin olive oil

4 garlic cloves, smashed

8 ounces chopped carrot

8 ounces chopped yellow onion

8 ounces chopped celery

1 quart chicken stock

1 ounce tomato paste

1 ounce all-purpose flour

PANISSE

2 quarts water

1.2 ounces salt

16 ounces chickpea flour, plus more for tossing

3 quarts vegetable oil, for frying

Salt

3 ounces dried Black Mission figs, julienned

1 cup freshly grated Manchego cheese

0.5 ounce minced fresh chives

OSSO BUCCO Preheat the oven to 275°F. Season the osso bucco with salt and pepper, then sear in the oil in a Dutch oven over high heat until brown on all sides.

Remove the veal, add the vegetables and cook for 15 to 20 minutes until deeply caramelized. Deglaze with spoonfuls of the chicken stock occasionally so the bottom doesn't burn.

Add the tomato paste and cook for 2 to 3 minutes until deep reddish-brown. Add the flour and stir to incorporate.

Add the remaining stock and return the meat to the pot. Cover tightly and braise in the oven for about 80 minutes.

Remove from the oven; cover and refrigerate overnight.

Remove and discard the fat from the top of the pot. Shred the meat into big chunks.

Pulse the meat and vegetables in a food processor until it just comes together. Add a little jus as you process to loosen the mixture if needed. Reserve the remaining jus for later.

CONTINUED >

PANISSE Boil the water in a large pot over high heat and add the salt. Slowly whisk in the chickpea flour, reduce the heat to low and cook for 5 minutes, stirring constantly.

Pour the batter onto a parchment-lined half sheet pan and spread it in an even layer using a spatula.

Refrigerate overnight. The next day, cut the panisse into 1½-inch rounds using a cookie cutter and toss them gently with more chickpea flour.

Place the floured panisse circles on another parchment-lined half sheet pan.

ASSEMBLY Heat the vegetable oil in the deep fryer to 350°F.

Reheat the osso bucco in some of the reserved jus and set aside.

Fry a few pieces of panisse for 2 minutes or until golden brown. Drain on a paper towel-lined plate and season with salt.

Top each piece of panisse with a spoonful of osso bucco, some julienned figs, a sprinkle of Manchego and a pinch of chives.

Serve immediately.

CHEF'S NOTES

SPECIAL TOOLS: Deep Fryer, Dutch Oven, 1½-Inch Round Cookie Cutter

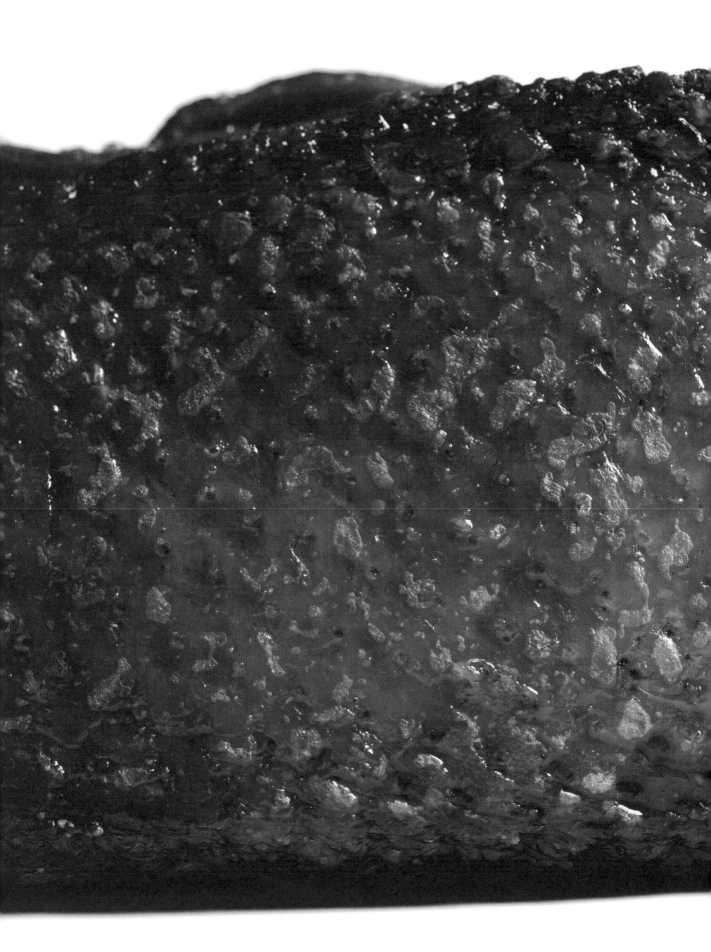

DUCK CONFIT QUESADILLAS

Makes 40 to 50 pieces

PICKLED CORN SALAD

3 ounces Pickled Corn (page 221)

3.5 ounces small-diced apple

2 teaspoons finely chopped flat-leaf parsley

1 tablespoon extra-virgin olive oil

DUCK LEG CONFIT

3 pounds duck legs

0.66 ounce salt

0.33 ounce sugar

2 quarts duck fat

FILLING

6 ounces caramelized onions

1 cup grated Parmesan cheese

6 tablespoons extra-virgin olive oil

Salt and freshly ground black pepper

6 (12-inch-diameter) flour tortillas

Extra-virgin olive oil

4 scallions, thinly sliced

PICKLED CORN SALAD Strain the corn, reserving 1 tablespoon of the pickling liquid. Place the corn and reserved pickling liquid in a large bowl, add the apples, parsley and extra-virgin olive oil, and toss well.

DUCK LEG CONFIT Toss the duck with the salt and sugar. Place in an airtight container and refrigerate overnight.

The next day, preheat the oven to 275°F. Place the duck legs in a Dutch oven along with the duck fat. Clip a candy thermometer to the inside of the pot and melt the fat over medium heat. When it reaches 150°F, cover the pot and transfer to the oven. Confit the duck for 2 to 2½ hours or until the meat pulls away from the bone, checking at the 90-minute mark to make sure that it isn't cooking faster than expected.

Remove the pot from the oven. Place the duck legs on a cutting board, let them cool, then remove all the meat from the bones.

FILLING Place the duck meat in a food processor along with the caramelized onions, Parmesan and olive oil. Pulse until combined, then taste and season with salt and pepper.

ASSEMBLY Preheat the oven to 350°F.

Using a 2-inch round biscuit or cookie cutter, punch 80 to 100 tortillas out of larger store-bought tortillas. Top half of the tortillas with a heaping 100 scoop (0.33 ounce) of the duck filling. Place a second tortilla on top.

Brush each quesadilla with extra-virgin olive oil, place on large baking sheets and toast in the oven for 3 to 4 minutes.

Remove from the oven, garnish each with 2 teaspoons of the pickled salad and some scallions and serve immediately.

CHEF'S NOTES

SPECIAL TOOLS: Dutch Oven, 2-Inch Round Biscuit or Cookie Cutter, 100 Scoop , Candy Thermometer

LAMB CHOPS

Makes 40 chops

FENNEL PURÉE

2 tablespoons vegetable oil

1.5 ounces sliced shallots

0.5 ounce smashed garlic

20 ounces diced fennel

2 cups whole milk

0.5 ounce salt

Freshly ground black pepper

FENNEL FROND CHIMICHURRI

4 ounces fennel fronds

1 ounce smashed garlic

1 ounce sliced shallots

1 cup red wine vinegar

1.5 ounces fresh parsley leaves

Crushed red pepper flakes

Salt

1½ cups extra-virgin olive oil

LAMB

4 ounces onion powder

3 ounces paprika

2 ounces dried rosemary

0.5 ounce freshly ground black pepper

4.5 ounces kosher salt

4 cups panko breadcrumbs

5 racks of lamb, frenched

2 cups Dijon mustard

FENNEL PURÉE Heat the oil in a large pot over medium heat and sauté the shallots and garlic for 2 to 3 minutes or until soft. Add the fennel and cook for 3 to 4 minutes, then pour in the milk and add the salt and pepper. Bring to a boil, reduce the heat to low, cover and simmer for 24 minutes. Strain the liquid through a fine-mesh sieve into a bowl. Place the solids in a blender. Purée until smooth, then add a little of the reserved liquid at a time until the mixture is silky smooth and the purée holds its shape when spooned onto a plate. Transfer to an airtight container and refrigerate until needed.

FENNEL FROND CHIMICHURRI Add all the ingredients except the oil to a blender. Purée on high speed until smooth, then, with the motor running, drizzle in the oil. Transfer to an airtight container and refrigerate until needed.

LAMB In a blender, combine the onion powder, paprika, rosemary, pepper and salt. Blend on high speed until the mixture is uniform in color, then add the panko and blend on high speed for 20 to 30 more seconds.

Slather each rack of lamb with a thin layer of Dijon on the top side of the loin. Generously dust with the seasoned panko and pat gently to press the panko into place. Cover and refrigerate.

Preheat the oven to 350°F. Place the lamb on large, rimmed baking sheets and roast for 8 to 10 minutes or until it reaches an internal temperature of 150°F. Remove the lamb from the oven and let it rest for 4 minutes, then slice into individual chops.

ASSEMBLY Swipe a spoonful of fennel purée on your serving platter and lay the individual chops on top. Drizzle with the chimichurri and serve immediately.

SPECK & BLACKBERRIES

Makes 40 to 50 pieces

9 ounces robiola cheese

13 very thin slices speck

50 (⅛-inch-thick, 2-inch-long) slices ficelle

25 blackberries, halved

½ cup (1 stick) unsalted butter

2 ounces honey

2 ounces fresh chervil leaves

Freeze the cheese for about 20 minutes and then slice it into squares about ⅛ inch thick. Lay out on a parchment-lined pan, without overlapping.

Cut each slice of speck once lengthwise and once down the middle so you have four 3-inch ribbon-like pieces. Reserve.

ASSEMBLY On each slice of ficelle, place a piece of cheese and a half blackberry.

Using a piece of speck, wrap around the bread, cheese and blackberry, so that the seam of the cured meat is on the bottom of the bread.

Finish the rest and set aside.

Heat a sauté pan over medium heat and add 1 table-spoon of butter. Place a few of the hors d'oeuvres seam-side down in the pan and cook for 2 minutes until the speck is crisp and the cheese is melted. Repeat with the remaining pieces, adding more butter as needed.

Remove, drizzle with honey and place a leaf of chervil on each.

Serve immediately.

FOIE MOUSSE ON APPLE CHIPS

Makes 50 pieces

FOIE MOUSSE

1 pound foie gras, sliced into ½-inch pieces

1¼ cups heavy cream

3.5 ounces salt

APPLE CHIPS

0.25 ounce fennel seeds

3 ounces granulated sugar

¼ cup water

2 tablespoons freshly squeezed lemon juice

6 Gala apples, cut into 1/16-inch-thick slices

FENNEL-APPLE COMPOTE

3 tablespoons extra-virgin olive oil

7 ounces fennel, cut into small dice

10 ounces Gala apples, peeled, cored and cut into small dice

¼ cup apple cider vinegar

2 ounces light brown sugar

0.2 ounce salt

½ cup toasted sliced almonds

Chive tips, for garnish

FOIE MOUSSE Heat a large skillet over high heat. Sear the foie gras in the hot pan for 1 minute, then flip and cook for 1 more minute.

Transfer the foie gras to a blender, add the cream and salt, and blend on high speed until smooth. Spoon the mixture into an iSi canister with one charge. Charge only when ready to use. Keep at 70°F.

APPLE CHIPS Preheat the oven to 275°F.

Toast the fennel seeds in a medium saucepan over medium heat for 30 seconds. Add the granulated sugar, water and lemon juice and bring to a boil. Let the mixture boil until the sugar is fully dissolved, then remove the pan from the heat and let it cool to room temperature.

Dip the apple slices into the cooled syrup and arrange them in a single layer on a Silpat. Dehydrate the apples in the oven for 50 minutes. Remove from the oven.

FENNEL-APPLE COMPOTE Heat the oil in a large saucepan over medium heat and sauté the fennel and apple for 3 minutes or until soft. Add the vinegar, brown sugar and salt and cook for 5 more minutes until syrupy. Let the compote cool to room temperature, then transfer it to an airtight container and refrigerate until needed.

ASSEMBLY On each apple chip, place some foie mousse, 1 tablespoon of the compote and a sprinkle of sliced almonds. Garnish with chive tips. Serve immediately.

CHEF'S NOTES

Working with foie gras is for the experienced chef.

SPECIAL TOOLS: Silpat, iSi Canister

CHAPTER TEN

COCKTAILS

Cocktails can be so personal. My first date with Erica began over a couple of Dark 'n Stormys in a small, poorly lit Manhattan hotspot. It seemed only appropriate that we served these at our wedding as our signature drink.

Everyone has a story to tell and, oftentimes, we're brought into the fold of making that happen for our clients. A signature cocktail is a great way to give an event personality. Guests love customizing them, the names are always quirky and it's an excuse to drink something more interesting and delicious than you may normally choose.

As we do with our food, we take our beverages just as seriously. They need to be seasonal, the client needs to love it conceptually and they need to taste fantastic.

FIG BOURBON SMASH

Makes 1 cocktail

1 brown sugar cube

3 or 4 dashes Angostura orange bitters

1 tablespoon fig jam, homemade (recipe follows) or store-bought

1 lemon wedge

2.5 fluid ounces high-quality Kentucky bourbon

Splash of filtered water

GLASS: rocks/old fashioned

ICE: 1 extra-large ice sphere

GARNISH: lemon slice

PAIRING: Foie Mousse on Apple Chips (page 193), Osso Bucco on Panisse (page 181)

Place the sugar cube in an old fashioned glass. Dash the bitters directly onto the sugar. Add the fig jam and lemon wedge and muddle until the sugar is completely dissolved. Add the ice sphere to the glass and slowly drizzle the bourbon over the ice. Add water, stir, and serve with a lemon slice.

FIG JAM
Makes 1½ cups

12 dried Black Mission figs

½ cup sugar

½ cup filtered water

3 tablespoons cranberry juice

Juice of ½ lemon

Add the figs, sugar, water and cranberry juice to a small pot. Bring to a boil, stirring occasionally, to dissolve the sugar evenly. Reduce the heat and simmer for 5 minutes. Remove from the heat and allow to cool.

Add the fig mixture and lemon juice to a food processor. Pulse until smooth.

Chill in your jar of choice in the refrigerator.

_____

CHEF'S NOTES

Bourbon is the star of this cocktail, so be sure to use a high-quality brand.

Our fig jam isn't just for drinks! Serve alongside your favorite cheeses on a charcuterie board.

CHAMOMILE SPARKLER

Makes 1 cocktail

1 fluid ounce chilled Chamomile Honey Syrup
(recipe follows)

5 fluid ounces chilled prosecco

GLASS: stemless flute or champagne coupe

ICE: none

GARNISH: lemon peel

PAIRING: Micro Latkes with Caviar and Crème
Fraîche (page 109), Fritto Misto (page 68)

Add the honey syrup to a chilled champagne coupe.
Pour in the prosecco and rub the lemon peel around
the lip of the glass. Squeeze the peel over the finished
cocktail to release the lemon's natural oils, and drop it
into the finished beverage.

CHAMOMILE HONEY SYRUP

Makes ¾ cup

1 chamomile tea bag (Harney and Sons)

6 fluid ounces hot filtered water

3 tablespoons honey

1 lemon rind, peeled into strips

In a small saucepan, steep the chamomile tea in the
hot water for 5 minutes. Remove the tea bag and add
the honey and half of the lemon peels, reserving the
other half for garnish. Bring to a boil over medium-
high heat, then reduce the heat to medium-low and
simmer for 20 minutes or until the liquid has reduced
by half. Remove the saucepan from the heat and let
the syrup cool to room temperature, then cover and
refrigerate until chilled.

COLD AND STORMY

Makes 1 cocktail

1.5 fluid ounces Pear-Infused Rum (recipe follows)

2 fluid ounces Ginger Beer (page 202)

0.5 fluid ounce freshly squeezed lime juice

GLASS: stemless martini glass or copper Moscow Mule mug

ICE: classic ice cubes

GARNISH: pear slice, lime peel, edible flower

PAIRING: Duck Confit Quesadillas (page 186), Braised Short Rib on Crispy Potatoes (page 115)

Fill the mug with 1 cup of ice. Add the rum, ginger beer and lime juice; stir. Garnish with a pear slice, lime peel and edible flower and serve.

PEAR-INFUSED RUM

Makes 3⅛ cups

8 ripe pears (any variety), quartered

1 whole vanilla bean, split

1 (750-ml) bottle white rum

Place the cut pears and split vanilla bean in a gallon-size mason jar and pour in the rum. Seal the lid tightly and store it in a cool, dry place for 1 to 2 weeks, turning the jar every other day or so. Once the rum is done infusing, strain it through a fine-mesh sieve into a large glass bottle with a tight-fitting lid. It will keep in the refrigerator for up to 1 month. The rum can be stored in the freezer for 3 to 6 months.

CHEF'S NOTES

If you don't want to make your own ginger beer, use store-bought instead. The classic choice is Goslings.

Pear nectar can be used with white rum as a substitution for pear-infused rum. Pear-flavored vodka will also work in this recipe.

JACK AND GINGER JULEP

Makes 1 cocktail

10 fresh mint leaves

½ lime, quartered

1 teaspoon sugar

2 fluid ounces Ginger Beer (recipe follows)

1.5 fluid ounces Jack Daniel's or Woodford Reserve whiskey

Splash of seltzer

GLASS: silver julep cup

ICE: crushed

GARNISH: fresh mint leaves

PAIRING: BBQ Brisket Po'Boys (page 165), Crab Toasts (page 125), Chicken and Waffles (page 83)

Place the mint, lime and sugar in a julep cup. Muddle until the leaves begin to break down, then pour in the ginger beer. Fill the glass three-quarters full with crushed ice. Add the whiskey and top with the seltzer. Stir and garnish with mint.

GINGER BEER

Makes 1¾ cups

½ cup packed dark brown sugar

2 cups filtered water

4 to 5 ounces fresh ginger, peeled and chopped

1 large stalk lemongrass, chopped

½ jalapeño pepper with seeds intact

Juice of 1 lime

In a medium saucepan over medium heat, dissolve the brown sugar in the water. Add the ginger, lemongrass and jalapeño and bring to a boil. Reduce the heat to low and simmer for 15 to 20 minutes. Remove the pan from the heat and allow the syrup to cool slightly, then strain it through a fine-mesh sieve into a jar with a lid, pushing on the solids to extract as much liquid as possible. Let it cool to room temperature, then pour in the lime juice. Seal and refrigerate until chilled.

SOUTH END MARTINI

Makes 1 cocktail

1 lemon, cut into small wedges

10 fresh mint leaves

2 teaspoons sugar

1 cup ice cubes

2 fluid ounces citrus-flavored vodka

1 egg white

GLASS: stemless martini glass

ICE: none

GARNISH: none

PAIRING: Jicama Wraps (page 12), Fish and Chips
(page 119), Steak Frites (page 120)

Place the lemon, mint and sugar in a cocktail shaker.
Muddle until the mint begins to break down and the
sugar is dissolved. Add the ice to the shaker followed
by the vodka and egg white. Cap and shake for
30 seconds. Strain into a chilled martini glass.

CHEF'S NOTES

The egg white will give the cocktail a creamy, silky
texture that will feel rich on the tongue.

STRAWBERRY-BASIL CAIPIRINHA

Makes 1 cocktail

3 strawberries, hulled and quartered

¼ lime, cut into wedges

2 fresh basil leaves

0.5 fluid ounce Strawberry-Balsamic Shrub (recipe follows)

1.5 fluid ounces cachaça

GLASS: highball or Collins

ICE: shaved or small square cubes

GARNISH: basil sprig, strawberry

PAIRING: Shrimp Ceviche (page 26), Blackened Cod Tacos (page 15)

In a highball or Collins glass, combine the strawberries, lime, basil and shrub. Muddle until the strawberries and basil are completely broken down. Fill the glass three-quarters full with ice. Add the cachaça, stir, garnish with the basil sprig and strawberry and enjoy.

STRAWBERRY-BALSAMIC SHRUB

Makes 3 cups

2 cups hulled and chopped strawberries

2 cups high-quality aged balsamic vinegar

2 cups sugar

Combine all the ingredients in a mixing bowl and stir until the sugar is dissolved. Cover with plastic wrap and refrigerate for 5 to 8 days, stirring occasionally. Give it a taste. If the mixture seems too acidic, add more sugar in spoonfuls as needed.

Strain the shrub through a fine-mesh sieve into a bottle with a lid, extracting as much liquid as possible. Discard the solids. Seal and store the shrub in the fridge for up to 6 months. Shake before using.

CHEF'S NOTES

Add a splash of the shrub to club soda for a refreshing nonalcoholic drink, or drizzle it over vanilla ice cream.

BEGINNINGS

206

TEQUILA ESPECIADO

Makes 1 cocktail

Makes 1 cocktail

1 tablespoon kosher salt

1 teaspoon chili powder

1 lemon wedge

1 cup ice cubes

2 fluid ounces Chile-Spiced Apple Cider
(recipe follows)

2 fluid ounces tequila

0.5 fluid ounce freshly squeezed lemon juice

GLASS: margarita or decorative rocks glass

ICE: blended

GARNISH: apple wedge, chili salt rim

PAIRING: Jicama Wraps (page 12), Steak Tostadas
(page 177)

In a shallow bowl, mix together the salt and chili powder.

Rub the lemon wedge along half the rim of the glass.
Dip the glass into the chili powder–salt mixture,
allowing the salt to stick to the wet portion of the rim.
Set aside.

Place the ice in a blender and add the spiced cider,
tequila and lemon juice. Pulse to break up the ice and
then blend until smooth. Pour into the rimmed glass
and garnish with the apple wedge. Serve immediately.

CHILE-SPICED APPLE CIDER

Makes 1¾ cups

2 cups fresh-pressed apple cider

1-inch piece fresh ginger, peeled and chopped

1 cinnamon stick

1 dried red chile, halved

Combine all the ingredients in a medium saucepan and
bring the mixture to a boil over high heat. Reduce the
heat to low and simmer for 20 minutes. Remove the
pan from the heat and let the syrup cool slightly, then
strain it through a fine-mesh sieve into a bottle with a
lid. Seal and refrigerate for up to 2 weeks.

CHEF'S NOTES

Add seltzer to your spiced cider and pour it over
vanilla ice cream for a zesty ice cream float!

ONTHEMARC
RECIPES

BÉCHAMEL

Makes 1 quart

1 quart whole milk
4 tablespoons unsalted butter
2 ounces all-purpose flour
Salt

Warm the milk in a medium saucepan over low heat until it comes to a bare simmer; keep it warm on the stovetop.

In a second saucepan, melt the butter over medium heat and dump in the flour. Stir until incorporated, then cook for 3 to 4 minutes, stirring constantly, until the roux changes to a blond color and smells nutty.

Whisk in the warm milk 1 cup at a time, fully incorporating it before adding the next cup. Once all the milk is added, bring the béchamel just to a boil over medium heat, stirring frequently to prevent sticking.

Remove the pan from the heat, season with salt and transfer to an airtight container. Set aside.

CHEF'S NOTE

A hot pot can still scorch your béchamel, so once it is seasoned, transfer it to another container as soon as possible.

BBQ SAUCE

Makes 2 quarts

35 ounces ketchup, homemade (page 214) or store-bought
⅓ cup water
¼ cup apple cider vinegar
2.5 ounces light brown sugar
0.35 ounce mustard powder
0.25 ounce onion powder
0.25 ounce garlic powder
Pinch of cayenne pepper
26 ounces frozen peaches

Combine everything in a large pot and cook uncovered over low heat, stirring often, for about 1 hour or until thickened.

Remove the pot from the heat and let it cool slightly, then blend the sauce with a stick blender until smooth.

Cool, transfer to an airtight container and store in the refrigerator for up to 2 weeks.

BLACK PEPPER GRAVY

Makes 4 cups

2 ounces butter
2 ounces all-purpose flour
4 cups milk, divided
2 teaspoons coarsely ground black pepper

Melt the butter in a small saucepot over low heat. Sprinkle the flour into the butter and incorporate with a spatula. Stir over low heat for 4 to 5 minutes until the roux smells nutty and has changed color. Turn the heat to medium. Whisk in 1 cup of the milk and allow to thicken. Add the second cup of milk and allow to thicken, stirring often. Repeat for the remaining 2 cups of milk. When finished and the mixture is thick, stir in the black pepper. Cover the pot and reserve over very low heat. Stir every 5 or 6 minutes to prevent scorching.

___

CHEF'S NOTE

A hot pot can still scorch your gravy, so once it is seasoned, transfer it to another container as soon as possible.

HUMMUS

Makes 1½ quarts

1 pound dried chickpeas
3⅓ teaspoons baking soda, divided
1 cup and 2 tablespoons lemon juice
2 cloves garlic
4 teaspoons salt
1 cup tahini
1½ teaspoons cumin

Soak the chickpeas in water with half the baking soda for 12 or more hours. Drain the chickpeas and rinse. Place in a pot with new water and the remaining baking soda. Simmer until extremely tender, about 50 minutes. In a blender, blend the lemon juice, garlic and salt. Let sit for 10 minutes and then strain. In a food processor, combine the tahini, cumin and lemon juice mixture and process for 4 minutes. Add the warm chickpeas and season to taste with salt. Blend until very smooth using the tamper as you go.

ONTHEMARC SIGNATURE KETCHUP

Makes 1 quart

0.7 ounce vegetable oil

7.5 ounces finely diced yellow onion

0.45 ounce minced garlic

0.1 ounce chili powder

0.05 ounce paprika

0.02 ounce ground cinnamon

0.02 ounce ground allspice

2 ounces honey

0.55 ounce tomato paste

2.95 ounces light brown sugar

3.85 ounces apple cider vinegar

27.6 ounces crushed tomatoes

0.25 ounce kosher salt

3 ounces extra-virgin olive oil

Heat the vegetable oil in a medium saucepan over medium heat. Add the onion and cook for 2 minutes or until translucent, then add the garlic and sauté just until fragrant, 30 to 45 seconds. Add the chili powder, paprika, cinnamon and allspice to the pan and sauté until fragrant, 15 to 20 seconds. Stir in the honey and tomato paste, cook for 2 to 3 minutes, and finally add the sugar, vinegar, crushed tomatoes and salt. Bring the mixture to a boil, then reduce the heat to low and simmer uncovered for 90 minutes, stirring occasionally, until the sauce has thickened. Remove the ketchup from the heat and let it cool slightly, then spoon it into a food processor and drizzle in the olive oil while blending on high speed.

Let the ketchup cool completely, then transfer it to an airtight container and store it in the refrigerator for up to 2 weeks.

HOMEMADE MAYONNAISE

Makes 1 quart

1 garlic clove

2 tablespoons freshly squeezed lemon juice

0.125 ounce kosher salt

0.25 ounce Dijon mustard

1 drop extra-virgin olive oil

⅓ cup ice

2 whole eggs

2⅔ cups vegetable oil

Combine everything except the vegetable oil in a blender and pulse a couple of times to loosely mix and break up the ice.

Turn the blender to high and drizzle the vegetable oil through the feed tube at a steady pace until the mayonnaise is smooth and emulsified.

VARIATIONS

(Based on one batch of Homemade Mayonnaise unless otherwise noted.)

SPICY MAYO: Mix in 7 ounces sriracha and salt to taste.

GOCHUJANG MAYO: Mix in 2 ounces gochujang, ¼ cup lime juice and 2 tablespoons fish sauce.

CAJUN AIOLI: Mix in 1.5 ounces Blackening Seasoning (pages 222), ⅓ ounce smoked paprika, the zest of 2 limes and ¼ cup lime juice.

LEMON AIOLI: Mix in the zest of 2 lemons.

REMOULADE: Into 3 cups of Homemade Mayonnaise, mix in 8 teaspoons mustard, 2 tablespoons apple cider vinegar, 4 tablespoons chopped parsley, 4 thinly sliced scallions and 1 tablespoon chopped capers.

TOMATO JAM

Makes about 2 cups

1 tablespoon vegetable oil
6 ounces sliced yellow onion
2 garlic cloves, smashed
36.5 ounces crushed tomatoes
¼ cup sugar
¼ cup extra-virgin olive oil
Salt to taste
Sherry vinegar to taste

Place a medium sauté pan over medium heat and add the vegetable oil, onion and garlic.

Cook for 4 to 5 minutes, stirring occasionally, then add the crushed tomatoes and sugar.

Bring to a boil and then reduce to a bare simmer over very low heat.

Cook for 90 minutes, stirring occasionally, or until the jam doesn't immediately come back together when you drag a spoon through it.

Transfer the jam to a blender, add the olive oil and blend on low speed until incorporated.

Taste and season with salt and sherry vinegar, let it cool to room temperature and transfer it to an airtight container. The jam will keep in the refrigerator for up to 1 month.

POULTRY BRINE

Makes 1 gallon

3 quarts plus 1 cup water
¾ cup kosher salt
2 tablespoons coriander seeds
1 tablespoon whole black peppercorns
2 tablespoons mustard seeds
1 lemon, halved
¼ medium red onion
1 bay leaf
1 garlic clove, crushed
32 ounces ice cubes

In a large pot, combine all the ingredients except the ice, and bring to a boil over high heat.

Once the brine reaches a rolling boil, strain it through a fine-mesh sieve or colander into a heatproof container and add the ice.

Allow the brine to cool to room temperature before using.

POTATO CHIPS

Makes 50 to 60 chips

3 quarts vegetable oil, for frying
3 large russet potatoes, cut into ¹⁄₁₆-inch-thick slices
1 cup white distilled vinegar
Salt

Heat the oil in your deep fryer to 325°F. Place the potatoes in a heatproof container.

Bring 1 gallon of water to a boil in a large stockpot and add the vinegar.

Cook the potatoes for 5 to 6 minutes until floppy and translucent but still firm and holding together.

Transfer the potatoes to a large colander and let them drain in the kitchen sink for 10 minutes, then fry them in batches for 5 to 6 minutes and drain them on a wire rack.

The chips will be light golden brown, just like your favorite kettle-cooked chips. Season with salt to taste.

TUILES

Makes approximately 50 tuiles

⅓ cup sugar
4 egg whites
2 tablespoons white miso
¼ cup melted unsalted butter
½ cup all-purpose flour
½ cup sesame seeds, toasted

Preheat the oven to 275°F, no fan.

In the bowl of a stand mixer fitted with the whisk attachment, whip the sugar and egg whites on high speed just until soft peaks begin to form.

In a separate bowl, stir together the miso and melted butter. Pour this mixture into the bowl with the egg whites and beat on medium speed until combined.

Whisk in the flour by hand until the batter is completely smooth, and then allow it to rest for 20 minutes.

Line a large rimmed baking sheet with a silicone baking mat. Using a squeeze bottle, squeeze 2-inch drops of the batter onto the prepared pan, spacing the drops about ½ inch apart. The batter will spread a little bit, so pour carefully. Scatter the sesame seeds over the top.

Transfer the baking sheet to the oven and bake for 10 to 12 minutes or until the tuiles are light golden brown all over.

Remove the pan from the oven and, using a spatula, transfer the tuiles to a cool dish.

Once cool, transfer the tuiles to an airtight container and store them at room temperature until needed.

FLATBREADS

Makes 6 large (approximately 2 x 12-inch)
flatbreads

1 pound "oo" flour

2 tablespoons extra-virgin olive oil

0.25 ounce kosher salt

0.25 ounce active dry yeast

0.5 ounce sugar

1 cup warm water

Add the flour, oil and salt to the bowl of a stand mixer fitted with the dough hook attachment.

In a separate bowl, whisk together the yeast, sugar and water until the yeast and sugar are fully dissolved. Set aside for 10 minutes or until a frothy layer forms on top.

Add the wet ingredients to the dry ingredients in the mixer and mix on the lowest setting for 5 minutes or until the dough is smooth.

Divide the dough into 6 equal-size balls and place them on a lightly floured countertop or cutting board in a warm place. Cover the dough balls with a clean, damp kitchen towel and allow them to rest until they have doubled in size, about 90 minutes.

Once the dough has doubled in size, take a piece and stretch it with your hands into a 2 x 6-inch rectangle. Then, using a rolling pin, roll the dough to a $\frac{1}{16}$-inch thickness. Preheat a grill to high.

Grill for about 1 minute per side and immediately transfer the flatbread to a wire rack to cool. Repeat with the remaining dough.

BASIC PÂTE À CHOUX

Makes 50 slider-sized buns

2 cups water
2 cups whole milk
½ cup (1 stick) unsalted butter
0.5 ounce salt
4 cups all-purpose flour
1 dozen eggs

Preheat the oven to 300°F. Line 2 half sheet pans with parchment paper. Bring a small saucepan of water to a boil.

In a wide, tall pot, combine the water, milk, butter and salt and bring to a boil over medium-high heat, stirring occasionally. When the mixture begins to boil, add the flour, turn the heat to low and stir with a wooden spoon until a sticky dough begins to form.

Keep stirring until the dough pulls away from the sides of the pot and comes together into a ball. Remove the pot from the heat and transfer the dough to the bowl of a stand mixer fitted with the paddle attachment. Beat the dough on the lowest speed for 5 minutes or until it has cooled slightly.

Meanwhile, crack all the eggs into a medium bowl.

After the dough has cooled down, turn the mixer to medium speed and begin to add the eggs one at a time, making sure that each egg is fully incorporated before adding the next. After you've added 6 of the eggs, stop to scrape down the sides of the bowl before continuing. Incorporate the remainder of the eggs, still adding them one at a time, until all of the eggs have been incorporated.

Dip a 2-ounce ice cream scoop into the boiling water and scoop balls of the dough onto the prepared baking sheets, spacing them 1 inch apart on all sides.

With wet hands, squish the balls down a bit and then bake them for 10 to 12 minutes or until golden brown all over. Remove the buns from the oven and let them cool to room temperature.

VARIATIONS

BACON: Replace the butter with bacon fat, in equal measure.

POPPY: Prior to baking and while the dough is moist, sprinkle poppy seeds over the top (⅓ cup poppy seeds for one recipe of choux).

DILL: Add ¼ cup finely chopped dill to the choux dough just before scooping to bake. Place a beautiful dill piece on top of each bun for garnish.

CORN: Replace half of the flour with cornmeal, in equal measure.

PAPRIKA: Add 4 tablespoons smoked sweet paprika to the choux dough just before scooping to bake. Sprinkle a bit of paprika on the top of each bun for garnish.

MINIS: Use a 1-ounce scoop to make tinier buns, yielding 100 buns.

PICKLING LIQUID

Makes about 12 cups

1 cup sugar

½ cup kosher salt

6 cups water

2 cups rice wine vinegar

2 cups white vinegar

1 teaspoon coriander seeds

1 teaspoon crushed red pepper flakes

1 bay leaf

1 teaspoon mustard seeds

1 teaspoon fennel seeds

1 teaspoon whole black peppercorns

In a medium saucepan, combine the sugar, salt, water, rice wine vinegar, white vinegar, coriander seeds, red pepper flakes, bay leaf, mustard seeds, fennel seeds and peppercorns. Bring the mixture to a boil over high heat, then immediately strain it through a fine-mesh sieve into a container. Let cool to room temperature, then refrigerate until needed. Proceed with your recipe of choice to use the pickling liquid.

PICKLED CUCUMBERS

Makes 50 to 60 pickle slices

1 English cucumber, cut into $\frac{1}{16}$-inch slices using a mandoline

1 recipe Pickling Liquid (at left)

Pack the pickle ingredients into a large canning jar or other heatproof container with a lid. In a pot, bring the pickling liquid to a boil, then strain the liquid through a fine-mesh sieve into the jar with the cucumbers. Let cool to room temperature, then seal the jar and store it in the refrigerator until needed.

PICKLED BEETS

Makes 6 ounces

6 ounces cooked beets (see page 151), skinned
and julienned
½ cup chopped fresh flat-leaf parsley
½ recipe Pickling Liquid (page 219)

Combine the beets with the parsley, and then pickle
the mixture according to the Pickled Cucumbers
recipe on page 219.

PICKLED BLUEBERRIES

Makes 1 pint

1 pint fresh blueberries
¼ recipe Pickling Liquid (page 219)

Pickle the blueberries according to the Pickled
Cucumbers recipe on page 219.

PICKLED CARROTS

Makes 1 pint

1 large carrot, julienned
¼ recipe Pickling Liquid (page 219)

Pickle the carrots according to the Pickled Cucumbers
recipe on page 219.

PICKLED KUMQUAT

Makes 1 cup

10 fresh kumquats, cut into ¹⁄₁₆-inch rounds using
a mandoline
½ recipe Pickling Liquid (page 219)

Pickle the kumquats according to the Pickled Cucumbers recipe on page 219.

PICKLED RADISHES

Makes 1 quart

8 ounces breakfast radishes, cut into ⅟₁₆-inch slices using a mandoline
½ recipe Pickling Liquid (page 219)

Pickle the radishes according to the Pickled Cucumbers recipe on page 219.

PICKLED RED ONIONS

Makes 1 quart

2 medium red onions, thinly sliced
1 recipe Pickling Liquid (page 219)

Pickle the onions according to the Pickled Cucumbers recipe on page 219.

PICKLED SHALLOTS

Makes 1 pint

8 shallots, thinly sliced
¼ recipe Pickling Liquid (page 219)

Pickle the shallots according to the Pickled Cucumbers recipe on page 219.

PICKLED CORN

Makes 1 pint

1 pint fresh corn kernels
¼ recipe Pickling Liquid (page 219)

Pickle the corn according to the Pickled Cucumbers recipe on page 219.

BLACKENING SEASONING

Makes about 3 cups

4.5 ounces paprika

1 ounce dried thyme

2.7 ounces garlic powder

2.2 ounces onion powder

4.6 ounces sugar

2.75 ounces salt

1.75 ounces freshly ground black pepper

1.1 ounces cayenne pepper

0.2 ounce dried oregano

2 ounces ground cumin

0.45 ounce ground nutmeg

Combine all the ingredients in a mixing bowl and whisk together until fully incorporated. Transfer the seasoning mix to an airtight container and store it at room temperature.

BBQ RUB

Makes 1 quart

14 ounces sugar

3.5 ounces kosher salt

0.7 ounce freshly ground black pepper

0.05 ounce cayenne pepper

0.35 ounce chili powder

5.3 ounces onion powder

5.3 ounces garlic powder

10.6 ounces paprika

Combine all the ingredients in a medium bowl and whisk until everything is incorporated. Transfer the seasoning mix to an airtight container and store it at room temperature.

MEXICAN SEASONING

Makes 1 quart

1 cup granulated sugar

1 cup light brown sugar

⅓ cup salt

½ cup freshly ground black pepper

½ cup fennel seeds

2 cups coriander seeds

½ cup cumin seeds

2 pinches of chili powder

Combine all the ingredients in a medium bowl and whisk until everything is incorporated. Transfer the seasoning mix to an airtight container and store it at room temperature.

VADOUVAN SPICE BLEND

Makes 1 pint

⅔ pound yellow onions, cut into large dice

⅓ pound shallots, halved

4 garlic cloves

2 tablespoons vegetable oil

⅓ teaspoon fenugreek seeds

1 curry leaf, finely chopped

1 teaspoon ground cumin

⅓ teaspoon ground cardamom

⅓ teaspoon mustard seeds

¼ teaspoon ground turmeric

⅛ teaspoon ground nutmeg

⅛ teaspoon crushed red pepper flakes

Pinch of ground cloves

⅓ teaspoon freshly ground black pepper

Preheat the oven to 250°F, no fan.

Combine the onion, shallot and garlic in a food processor and pulse until they are finely chopped.

Heat the vegetable oil in a skillet over medium heat. Add the onion mixture and sauté for 25 minutes or until deep golden brown. Then mix in the remaining ingredients, transfer the mixture to a rimmed baking sheet and spread it out in a thin, even layer. Bake for 1 hour, stirring occasionally, or until the mixture is dried out but not burned. Once cool, transfer the seasoning mix to an airtight container and store it at room temperature.

_____

CHEF'S NOTE

Use this spice blend anywhere you would use madras curry powder; it's especially good on roasted vegetables!

DRY TEMPURA MIX

Makes about 3 cups (22.5 ounces)

20 ounces rice flour
0.38 ounce turmeric
1 ounce baking powder
0.6 ounce salt
0.5 ounce onion powder

Place all the ingredients in a large bowl and whisk well to combine.

CHEF'S NOTE

For best results, be very precise with these measurements.

TEMPURA BATTER

Makes 3¼ cups

1 pound Dry Tempura Mix (at left)
3 cups water

Place the tempura mix in a large bowl and whisk in the water. Set aside.

CRUNCHY TEMPURA

Makes 1 quart

3 quarts vegetable oil, for frying
½ recipe Tempura Batter (at left)

Heat the vegetable oil in your deep fryer to 350°F.

Slowly drizzle the tempura batter into the hot oil, being very careful so the oil doesn't boil over. Fry the tempura until it stops bubbling, then remove it with a slotted spoon and transfer it to a paper towel-lined plate to drain. Let the tempura cool to room temperature, then transfer it to an airtight container lined with paper towels.

ACKNOWLEDGMENTS

One of the things I find most gratifying in life is seeing an idea come to fruition. Creating a book is no small task. The outcome of the last two and a half years of highs, lows, laughs, and lulls has culminated in something of which I am irrevocably proud. Like many great accomplishments, there are a lot of people who must be acknowledged for helping this become a reality.

In alphabetical order:

AMANDA: Our beverage queen! Thank you for sharing your creativity and wisdom with the world. You were thrust into this experience and you handled it like a champion.

AMOS, XAVIER AND LISSELLY: When we told the photographer we were planning to shoot twenty dishes a day, he said that was unprecedented. For a group of people who had never created a cookbook before or taken food styling classes, you guys crushed it. You always exceed my expectations and I am most grateful for it.

AUNT RHONDA: Your legal knowledge and guidance have been crucial to the company's continued maturity. Thank you for always answering my questions and listening to my concerns throughout the years. You're not a bad Auntie, either!

CAITLIN: Your unique ability to take on a project and see it through to the end never ceases to amaze me. Where I would look at a task, see the enormity of what was in front of me and get bogged down, you see a large task and attack it with a composed, calm and steady force. My father always says that the last 5 percent of a project takes 95 percent of the time; in this case, that is, most definitely, the truth. Thank you for helping me realize this dream. Without your hard work and dedication to this project, we never would have made it across the finish line.

DAD: Not all young chefs are lucky enough to have an architect for a father. Thank you for all of your construction expertise through the years. It is much appreciated.

ERICA: I couldn't ask for a more supportive and loving companion. Whether I'm working every holiday, working at all hours or never committing to anything for fear of an event coming up, you are patient and kind and very understanding. Thank you for holding my hand while I chase my dreams.

THE FISHER FAMILY: Making soufflés during our late night Mario Kart parties was a great way to hone my skills. Thanks for being such great friends.

GRANNY RENA: Not a day goes by that I don't quote you or consider all that you have taught me. Thank you for sharing your wisdom with me.

IAN: You are always the second person I call when I need advice. (Don't let it go to your head because we all know runner-up is the first loser.) Thanks for all your time, patience and guidance over the years. Our brotherhood is built on mutual respect, which I realize is a rare thing to behold. Growing up with you was a distinct pleasure and growing old together, I hope, will be the same.

JIM M.: When we first met, I didn't understand how a vendor (you) could help a client (me) grow his business. After years of working together, I'd like to thank you for taking me under your wing and sharing your keen business insights with me. I learn something new from you each time we connect. Cheers to a continued collaboration.

JOANNE M: Thank you for helping me learn more about myself and for teaching me how to deal with the pressures of life in a healthy and enduring way.

JOHN LEE: You are a rockstar. Thank you for flying 3,000 miles and shooting four 10-hour days straight to capture the beauty of our food.

LAUREN: No matter how much I put on your plate, you handle it with a smile. Thank you for making work fun and for being my brain while my head is in the clouds.

THE LINHART FAMILY: Who would have thought that your five-course, ten-person dinner parties would turn into galas for over 700! Thank you for taking a chance on me at such a young age.

MICHAEL AND MARGERY KATZ: Thank you for your constant love and support.

MOM AND DAD: Thank you for cultivating my love for food at a young age. I wouldn't be where I am today without your help, love and support.

POPPA MERVYN: Wisdom, clarity and confidence come to mind when I think of you. Thank you for guiding me through the infancy of my company. You are my sounding board and I am so grateful for all your guidance.

TAYLOR AND THE BRANDT FAMILY: Besides being great friends, you have all been so instrumental in helping me garner some of my best business partnerships. TY YLB'S

INDEX

BEGINNINGS

Marc's Mandlebroit

1 cup oil	1 tablespoon oil
1 cup sugar	3 eggs, beaten
1 teaspoon vanilla abstract	2 cups flour
2 teaspoons baking powder	1 teaspoon salt
1 cups flour	1 tablespoon cocoa
1 tablespoon sugar	

If you want, you may add chocolate chips, M+M's or nuts, and the amount you put in does not matter.

To begin, preheat oven to 375 degrees. Then grease a cookie sheet with Pam or another kosher nonstick spray.

Now beat 1 cup oil, 1 tablespoon oil, 1 cup sugar and three beaten eggs. Beat this all until well combined in a large mixing bowl. Add 1 teaspoon vanilla abstract.

Combine 2 cups flour, 2 teaspoons baking powder and 1/2 teaspoon salt in a bowl. Gradually add this to the egg mixture.

If you chose to add chocolate chips, nuts or M+M's, now is the time.

Now we need to add the final cup of flour. Mix everything well. The dough will be stiff.

Drop the mixed batter into 2 rows across the cookie sheet. Sprinkle a mixture of cocoa and sugar on the top. Put the cookie sheet into the oven and bake for 20 minutes. Remove the cookie from the oven. Using a long serrared knife, slice the logs into 1/2 inch pieces and turn them on their sides. Place the sheet back in the oven for 15 minutes. Cool on racks and begin to eat.